LORD,
MAKE MY DAYS COUNT

LORD, MAKE MY DAYS COUNT

Ely Moskowitz

Philosophical Library
New York

Library of Congress Cataloging in Publication Data

Moskowitz, Ely.
Lord, make my days count.

1. Moskowitz, Ely. 2. Jews—United States—Biography.
I. Title.
E184.J5M7 1983   973'.04924024 [B]   83-2430
ISBN 0-8022-2423-7

Copyright © 1983, by Philosophical Library, Inc.
200 West 57th Street, New York, N. Y. 10019
All rights reserved
Manufactured in the United States of America

In loving memory of my illustrious parents:

Rabbi Charles Moskowitz, whose superb, logical mind so vividly reflected his accomplishments

Mother Rachel Moskowitz, an ultimate, providential symbol of utmost humanitarian generosity

a marital union so divinely blissful.

And also in memory of my immortal life partner Fannie, for those who ever met her could truly never forget her.

TABLE OF CONTENTS

Foreword   xi

I. *DECISIVE EVENTS*   1

    With My Father in the Country   5
    Teenage Love in my Bar Mitzvah Year   7
    1913, a Fateful Year   11

II. *ON THE WAY TO THE UNITED STATES*   18

    The Arrival of My Parents   23
    My Return to New York   25

III. *THE FATEFUL YEAR OF 1920*   27

    Perilous Courtship Days Ahead   29
    Our Honeymoon Week   38

Touring the East Side 41
Opening a Store 45
The Ominous Night of Birth 49
Drifting into a Dream 55
The Operation 59
Moving to Shamokin 61

IV. VENTURING IN REAL ESTATE 64

Darkening Skies 66
Assurance of a Friend 68
In the New Store 70
Fannie Begins Working in the Store 72
The Turbulent World Condition 73
The Closing of Mines 77
Depression Years 78
Excursions to New York 80
Entering the 1940s 84
My Brother Leaves for Hazleton 85
A Ray of Light amid Darkness 86
Wartime Rationing 90
War Ends—Myron Comes Home 93
The Medical School Frustration 96
Sister Arriving from England 100
The Postwar Years 103

V. THE MILLION-DOLLAR DIAMOND 106

Traveling Salesmen, A Breed in Themselves 108
The Night the Demons Feared 113
Merchants' Competition 115
Auctioneers on the Go 117
A Fortune an Auctioneer Missed 120

A Man Whose Fortune Strangers Inherited 122

VI. *THE CAVALCADE OF BLOOMING AND FADING COMMUNITIES* 125

Kosher Butcher Shops 127
The Rise and Decline 128
Shoeshine Parlors 130
Incidents of a Bygone Past 132
Minerva Was to Cure Patt 135
Poor Orders 138
Regional Doctors 140
General Practitioners 142

VII. *REGIONAL LAWYERS* 146

An Unusual Episode 149
The Attorney in Need of Shoes 151
Regional Politics 152
Episodes in a Political Campaign 157

VIII. *HIGH SCHOOL GRADUATIONS* 161

Supermarkets 164
My Sons' Bar Mitzvahs 166
Isaiah, Chapters 42 and 43 168

IX. *CARS IN MY LIFE* 172

Chess in My Life 178

X. FANNIE'S SERIOUS ILLNESS — 185

Celebrating Our Wedding Anniversary	189
Our Pilgrimage to Israel	189
Retiring from Business	191
Selling My Shamokin Store	193
My Retirement	194
My Father's Mother	196
Candle Lighting Sabbath Eve	197
Time to Reflect	198
Thoughts about Creation	201
Fannie's Death	202
Thoughts about Religion	204
Unbecoming Religious Friction	207
The Two Parts of the Jewish Religion	208
Ultimate Faith	209
The Essence of Religion	212

FOREWORD

During the course of my life I have often been reminded about the burning bush that Moses was confronted with. It was ablaze in a fiery conflageration yet could not be consumed.

It reflects so vividly the telltale, branded marks of my vulnerable life in which I miraculously surmounted fiery paths ultimately to share in the Almighty's gifts and blessings.

It was when I reached an advanced stage in my life that I began to see that the miracles and wonders were divinely meant to be my destiny.

I envisioned the times when imminent disaster truly seemed unavoidable and when decisions of life and death were made in grim moments of agonizing solitude.

I had often wondered how bridges suddenly appeared to cross turbulent rivers and how overpasses suddenly appeared to open fathomless chasms.

Surely, I thought, heavenly angels had been there to guide my way and light a torch to lead me to safety.

So this book is based on the marvelous events and episodes I experienced, and I am trying to portray them as they have actually taken place. I am presenting them in a panoramic outline against a vivid background of mankind's social, political, religious and personal behavior which so deeply penetrates and effects the very depths of the human spirit and soul.

Throughout the narration I emphasize the undeniable fact that, though a human being is a privileged entity endowed with freedom of choice, he is nevertheless largely motivated in his deeds and actions by a providential spiritual agitation which makes him worthy of being created in the Almighty's image.

It is for that reason I titled the book "Lord, Make My Days Count," as mankind's ultimate aim and purpose is not material but spiritual accomplishments which leave their worthwhile imprints in the sands of time.

So in my life there is not only an intuitive sense and instinct that I am embraced with the Lord's glorious presence, there is also the keen perception of the Almighty's countless, miraculous wonders that so joyfully imbued me with his blinding splendor.

I

Decisive Events

It was at the age of 16 that I left my birthplace in Russia, departing for my incomparable, providential home, the United States of America.

Because those priceless, formative, youthful years are so fundamental and meaningful in every person's life, I will briefly narrate the events of their development.

I first saw the light of day in the Autumn of 1898 in the metropolitan city of "Grodno."

It was the capital of the Grodno province, of whose nearly fifty thousand people more than half were Jewish.

From a tremendous tree-lined square in the center of the city, four streets radiated in their respective directions, forming thus a pivotal hub of commercial activities.

One of the more prestigious business streets emanating from the square was that named "Soborna," being an amalgamation of specialty stores as well as stores selling general merchandise.

One outstanding business establishment occupying a lucrative corner of the square and Soborna Street was that of "Muravyov," which was largely patronized by the aristocracy, high government officials and elite army personnel.

Gracing the shores of Grodno was the majestic "Nieman" river, whose navigational importance made it such a vital link to the Baltic Sea and an important outlet to Western Europe.

Its alluring historical past has deeply engrained itself in the heart of the people, and it was Napoleon's crossing with his army on his march to Moscow in 1812 that gave rise to many songs, legends and fantastic tales.

At a time when railroads dominated the economic and cultural life, Grodno was a pivotal hub from whose terminal one could make connections to Warsaw, Riga, Moscow and points west to Europe.

Being strategically an important link, it contained an extensive army base comprising more than forty thousand military personnel in its divisions.

Grodno was economically well situated according to the prevailing standards of the time.

It had numerous small industrial establishments, many qualified artisan workers, and expert craftsmen in numerous professions that drew a large clientele from far and wide.

But the main industry that provided a livelihood for thousands of residents was that of the Shereshewsky industrial plants, one of the largest cigarette manufacturing establishments in the Russian empire.

Not far from the town square, street after street leading down to the Nieman River was occupied by buildings and plants that treated and ground tobacco leaves and then packaged the finished product.

Its Number Ten brand was considered the most popular in Russia.

Nearly four hundred workers were employed just to make the boxes required for packing and distribution.

No less a factor in its economic development were the large army units stationed in the immediate confines of Grodno.

My parents had two stores dealing solely in the selling of herring; it was a poor man's basic and also a rich person's delicacy when prepared properly.

It provided us with a fairly comfortable livelihood and my father gave up a Rabbinical position so he could teach the multitude without any compensation. (The quotation in the Ethics of our fathers stating that one should not make the Torah like a shovel to earn a livelihood was constantly on his mind.)

It was in that conventional environment and mode of living that I started Cheder at the age of five and advanced to learn the Talmud a year ahead of time.

I once heard my Aunt Annie, my mother's sister, whispering to a neighbor, "Mark my word, Ely will be a Rabbi at sixteen."

That seemed to have made the rounds in the family circles until it must have been accepted as an unavoidable fact. Well, that is, until at the age of seven when in brief unforeseen seconds all seemed vanished like an elusive dream.

Two unusual episodes had to occur that warm July day to place me at the very spot where the danger of death threatened me so cruelly.

That was an era when animal power provided mankind's energy, but that July week the first example of miraculous automatic power to come was to be seen, its wonders to perform.

The governor of our Grodno province was a close friend of the Tsar and his Romanoff dynasty, immensely rich and always in the forefront of selfish innovations.

As a result, he was the first in the entire province, in fact in all the surrounding provinces, to purchase an automobile and lost no time driving it out on the main streets.

On that same day, a printing company had a sale on surplus waste paper, the kind which we used quite a lot in our stores to package the herring.

A man that usually does our errands went to help relatives to harvest on the farm, so I volunteered to carry some of the purchased paper to one of the stores that was badly in need of it.

With a roll of paper on my shoulder, I crossed a street just when the governor drove past in his car, continually sounding its horn.

Unaccustomed to that unusual wailing siren, the frightened horses of a wagon team raced away in a galloping stride striking me full force and disfiguring my face.

Being rendered instantly unconscious, I was rushed to a hospital where the doctors placed me on the critical list, the prognosis being considered poor.

For nearly three days I remained in a coma until I began gradually emerging into recovering wakefulness.

The doctors watched in amazement the astounding progress I made in my recovery, while my father attributed the sheer miracle to the many venerable Rabbis who came so often to pray for me.

Yet of one thing the doctors were certain, that since I had almost three days without oxygen, I could not escape considerable brain damage and some retardation.

I remained for about a month in the hospital where an ophthalmological specialist from Warsaw saved the sight of a damaged eye, with face and body cuts steadily healing, but with very little progress on my severely impaired mental condition.

Just before the near fatal accident I was one of the few school students who was far advanced in my Talmudical studies. Now as I left the hospital I could not even read the alphabetical letters.

My Aunt Annie, who proudly crowned me Rabbi at the forthcoming age of sixteen, was indeed totally heartbroken, but consoled herself that the Almighty had saved my life. "Boruch Hadoshem (God be blessed)," she kept on repeating.

With eight sisters and brothers home, it was always a beehive of activity, but with my presence in such deplorable condition, a most depressing mood now prevailed.

In the midst of such traumatic changes, it was my incomparable parents who held on courageously to the controlling helm, leading the family steadily back to the normal ways of active life.

Fortunate for myself was my father's decision to take personal charge of my mental rehabilitation, with his gifted psychological approach and logical wisdom truly proving my salvation.

Under his methodical, patient teaching, I learned the alphabet within several months and, by about the end of the winter season, began reading quite well.

It took me many years, though, to achieve the normalcy of an average student, and six years after the accident, when I was to celebrate my Bar Mitzvah day, I felt that my mind had finally reached my predestined base.

The well-known doctors in Grodno, Zamkow and Gushanski, who were professed atheists, began in later years to attend high holiday services and many contended that the miracle of my mental recuperation was greatly responsible for that.

WITH MY FATHER IN THE COUNTRY

Due to impaired lungs and other health conditions, my father would rent a small cottage in the countryside and remain there for several summer months.

During the last six years I was his sole companion, and when he would leave at times for a day or so to take care of some necessary business in Grodno, I ably managed to get along quite well.

Our cottage was in the depth of a virgin pine forest, with many such cabins and bungalows erected on its verdant hillsides.

At the panoramic foothills flowed a crystal-clear, meandering creek which cascaded to an onrushing waterfall that churned the wheels of a flour mill nestling in the valley.

I had my daily routine of learning, walking, and picking forest berries that grew there in such profusion, but it was the daily strolls I made with my father in the lanes of the verdant pine forest, and the cheerful chorus of singing birds that left a lasting impression in the years to come.

It was one endless lecture in religion and morality which was aimed at my mind.

Time and again my father kept on dwelling on the theme that a person consists of two parts, the physical and the spiritual.

"You well know, my son," he would emphasize, "that a person's body will cast a shadow whenever possible. The same holds true for the spiritual component, only in this instance it is the invisible form of a personal guiding angel.

"It is this guiding spiritual companion that intervened to save you from certain death and it will forever hasten to protect you in times of trouble and tribulation, if you do what is right for the creator and mankind."

Often stopping to gaze at me and note my reactions, he would determine whether he should continue his discourse or permit me to absorb the meaning of what had already been said.

At other times there was lecturing about ethics and morality, quoting the comments of the Rambam and other outstanding Talmudical authorities who left their lasting imprints in the annals of Jewish learning.

But it is a person's own accomplishments that in the long run account for the kind of life that molds his fate and destiny, my father would emphasize.

For some unaccountable reason, on those momentous strolls in the forest, he dwelt often on the dangerous pitfalls of feminine enticement.

He quoted extensively from the Bible and also from King Solomon's proverbs, and he eloquently related, sentence after sentence, the irresistible powers of sexual allurement and its captivating charm.

He probably realized that I was emerging from the age of boyhood to that of sexual interest and he probably felt that it wasn't too soon to make me conscious of it.

TEENAGE LOVE IN MY BAR MITZVAH YEAR

Indeed my father's perception came at a time when, in a way, I was about to be tested unexpectedly in the enticing realm of teenage emotions.

It happened one day when my father left in the morning for an omnibus that made its daily rounds between the Lasosne Resort and Grodno.

At a nearby cottage was a vacationing family of three that were our neighbors in a square where we lived in the city.

As it happened, the man and wife left that morning for Grodno, leaving their fourteen-year-old daughter in charge of the premises.

She was lean but seemingly athletically built, her blond, expressive face dominated by illuminative blue eyes while locks of wavy copper-red hair complimented her youthful attractiveness.

I often met her as she played in our courtyard with girl friends, going to school or doing errands for her parents, but neither of us seemed to take much note of each other.

Being somewhat yet a bit disfigured with some face scars, I was beset with an inferiority complex, and besides, my traditional orthodox training to avoid sexual temptation was a creed that had begun to dominate my life.

Strangely, the more I gave thought to the restrictions, the more I was at times provoked to ignore them, but I did indeed hold on to the line of my traditional upbringing and religious learning.

On that glorious day in July with my father away, I intended to take a stroll to a nearby field where a band of gypsies had recently camped when I saw my girl neighbor coming down the hill in my direction, holding something in her hands.

I waited a while and when I was certain that she was heading my way I courteously went to meet her.

"Are you all by yourself?" she asked in surprise.

"Yes, my father trusts me to behave well," I responded.

"So do my parents," she stated.

"Are they also away?" I inquired.

"Yes, they had to sign some papers and promised to return in the evening."

"I was just about to go up to the gypsy camp. You want to go along?" I summoned up the courage to invite her.

"Do you know they hypnotize people, steal children and perform magic?" she asked.

"Are you really afraid?" I earnestly asked her.

"My parents wouldn't like it and I don't feel like going there anyway," she said. "I brought you a piece of cake I baked myself, tell me what you think of it."

"I will probably commend you for its excellence even if it is not so perfect," I said.

"No, I want you to tell me the truth. You see, I am only a beginner, I don't expect miracles. Anyway, a Rabbi's son must tell the truth," she admonished me smiling.

"I promise to be fair," I said.

"Cake alone doesn't go well without a cold drink, you have some kwass (russian soda)?" she inquired.

"No, my father only drinks tea. The samovar (where tea is brewed) is always ready."

"No," she said, "I'll run up home and bring a bottle of kwass."

As she sprinted away, my heartbeats galloped in a maddening race while my quickening bloodstream flushed my face into a flaming inferno.

With the piece of cake in my hand, I waited for her return and decided we should share it together in our small kitchen which was next to the only other room in the house, used as a living room and bedroom.

Being confronted now by this fascinating girl in a gesture of friendship, I clearly realized how vulnerable I was at this developing age to the incitement of my inborn sexual urge.

She soon came back with a bottle of kwass and reached for glasses to pour it in.

She sat down next to me and, after cutting the cake, she mischievously held my hand while giving it to me.

Never being that close to any girl, especially one so fascinating, I was shocked by exciting emotions.

"Do you plan to be a Rabbi like your father?" she asked.

"It all depends on many things to follow," I said.

"I know your name, my mother told me the miracle of your recovery. My name is Shifra Nieman," she said as she moved closer with her knees touching mine.

Suddenly it dawned on me, the sin of being so close to a woman, and that, according to the sages, I was headed to the pitfalls of a fiery hell.

But this theoretical punishment I now sensed melting in an emotional transition so overwhelming and so thrilling and intoxicating.

In one way I somehow wished it would vanish like a dream, yet it was so thrilling I hoped there would be no end to this mysterious, captivating spell.

We kept on making conversation while my pulse beat ever faster, and Shifra impulsively moved closer to passionately embrace me, sealing it with a kiss that I ardently reciprocated in kind.

After some moments of somewhat embarrassing silence, Shifra said quietly, "This is the first kiss I ever gave any boy, and it isn't even the kind I give to my family." When she again kissed me passionately, I responded instinctively to nature's call to maturity.

Forgetting now all the tenets, creeds and laws about the sin of getting intimate with women and the fiery hell awaiting those who transgress its forbidden boundaries, I confessed to her that I too had now experienced the first kiss ever given any girl and, taking the courage to clasp her hands warmly, I added, "I too am glad it was you."

"This is the last week of vacation here for us. How about meeting you by the flour mill tomorrow?" she suggested.

I was about to give her my reply when we heard the sounds of footsteps on the porch.

We tried to calm ourselves while keeping a distance from each other. Soon, to our shock and surprise, in came my father. Even more than ours was my father's shock and surprise to see the refreshments on the table and the implications of our unexpected togetherness.

A bit flushed, Shifra said, "I baked a cake and thought of giving a piece to your son. You see, Rabbi Moskowitz, we are returning next week back to Grodno and I thought of treating him," she explained.

I knew my father's brilliant mind had perceived the true situation, but he left it for some other time to evaluate with me the moral lessons and the implications of what had occurred.

The same week the Nieman family's vacation was ending, but I was glad to have an opportunity to meet Shifra and to tell her how my father had missed the omnibus because of a changed schedule, and that maybe we would yet get together in Grodno.

But that youthful dream never materialized, for in October I celebrated my Bar Mitzvah and, soon after, I left to study in a Yeshivah (seminary) in a town many miles away from Grodno.

The Niemans too moved to a more residential section on Sodowa Street, miles away from where we lived, and that was the end of this brief, youthful infatuation which, like a flash of lightning, came and went in the elusive wonderland of youthful dreams.

Strangely I was also wishing and hoping that Shifra too would affectionately remember me.

For it was the first touch of youthful sexual awakening so inspiring in the golden age of blissful innocence.

1913, A FATEFUL YEAR

After celebrating my Bar Mitzvah in the year of 1911 my father lost no time arranging for me to leave for a prestigious Yeshivah established in the small town of Meretz.

My amazing mental recovery under his guidance was something that indeed elated him for I was again getting above average grades in Talmudic discourse and he was truly proud of it.

I once overheard my mother saying, "Maybe Aunt Annie is after all right and my Ely will excel as a Rabbi some day."

To my father, it also was a cherished ambition for me to continue the line of Rabbis in his venerable family.

Two years later, he arranged for me to enter a Yeshivah where his friend Simon Shcop, one of the most brilliant Talmudic scholars of the nineteenth century, was heading the teachers' faculty.

In early October of 1913 I left for the small town of Stuchin where the Yeshivah was located.

It was arranged for me to reside in the home of Malke Kalmens (Malke being her first name and Kalmen her father's name, the usual way to refer to someone in those times).

Malke Kalmens was a middle-aged widow living in a moderate home where fourteen other out-of-town students made themselves comfortable in the five-room dwelling.

That winter a scarlet fever epidemic went on the rampage and somehow it affected every student but me.

I left at once for Grodno, waiting for the scourge to abate and run its course.

One day during my return, my father went with me for morning services to a Synagogue where an eminent visiting Rabbinical sage was present.

Grodno had forty-one synagogues, some built by and for professional tradespeople like carpenters, tailors, hat makers, shoemakers and so on.

Others were for general membership, mostly businessmen and those in intellectual professions.

One that was erected by the common efforts of the entire Jewish population was known as the choir shull, truly an architectural wonder with a seating capacity of nearly six thousand.

The synagogue the eminent Rabbi was attending was named "Beth Hamedresh Hagodel" (great house of study), for it had continuous religious activities twenty-four hours a day. His name was "Israel Meyer Hachoen," but he was better known for the title of his famous book, "Chofetz Chaim" (purpose of life) stressing humanitarianism and divine morality.

All that morning there was a steady stream of visitors and worshippers who continually lined up to greet him and have the privilege of shaking the hand of this saintly man.

It was quite a while before my father had an opportunity to meet him for a more leisurely get-together, which he had wished for.

The Chofetz Chaim was a personal friend of my Uncle Joshua Zymbalist, an eminent Rabbi in the metropolitan city of Minsk, and was also well acquainted with my father, whom he had met several times before.

Greeting each other most affectionately, they entered into a lengthy conversation until at one point my father motioned for me to come over and introduced me to him.

Short of stature, wearing an ordinary cap denoting an inborn sense of humility, I now inadvertently saw in his hallowed countenance a radiant spiritual glow which was truly inspiring.

Serenely he inquired about my studies, the living conditions of the Yeshiva's students and faculty, and the progress I was making in my Talmudic learning.

Moving closer to me, his eyelids lowered, he put his hand on my head, murmured a silent prayer, and blessed me with the following Brocho (best wishes): "May the Almighty Creator of the universe forever guide you into a life of health, happiness in the sanctified realm and pathways of the Holy Torah."

Long after I left this glorious scene, I remembered the incisive gaze of a saintly man which had been deeply ingrained in my heart and soul.

Late that winter I returned to the Yeshivah in Stuchin to resume my studies, and one night I was captivated by a dream that lingered long in my mind.

I saw the Chofetz Chaim very vividly advising me to write without delay to my uncle in Pittsburgh to send me a travel ticket to get me to the United States.

As dreams go, this one too faded from my thoughts with the passing of time.

But within a matter of weeks, the same dream repeated itself in all its vivid details, making it so weirdly perplexing and yet meaningful.

Realizing my father's keen aspirations that I graduate as a Rabbi and that my departure to the States would mean an abortive end to that ambition, I knew that the decision of what to do had to be wholly my own.

For days I gave much thought to the unusual repetition of the dream in such exact detail, and the fact that the saintly Chofetz Chaim was the figure in the dream prompted me finally to send a letter to my uncle Abraham Isaac Silverman to ask him for a ticket.

To my amazing surprise, the following month I received a paid-up ticket which would take me all the way to Pittsburgh.

As I expected, my father reacted with distress to the thought of terminating my theological studies, but as I related the amazing dream time and time again, he relented and promised to help me in my departure plans.

And help was indeed indispensable in this situation, for at my age of sixteen, I was already subject to the military code and could not secure a passport to leave Russia.

Like many others in such a predicament, we secured the services of a smuggling agent skilled in the adventure of unauthorized border crossings.

One hot summer day in August, I made my rounds saying farewell to my family since they could not be present at the railroad station where a tumultuous departure would draw the attention of government officials.

Most agonizing was to part with my mother who, heartbroken, held onto me and fainted with my last, departing kiss.

Accompanying me to the railroad station and then on the train to my last stop at the town of Yogistov was my father.

There we left to follow the agent as per the pre-arranged instructions, and soon noted that we were joined by three boys and two girls. After a short walk we were directed to a corner home where the residing family was having its evening meal.

After my father was assured by the agent that everything was working out according to plan, I went outside and said farewell to him since he was to return home soon on a train for Grodno.

This last goodbye proved to be a most painful experience to endure.

For a while, we both remained in suspended silence as engulfing emotions seemed to make time stand still in its tracks.

For here I was to part, not only with a devoted, loving father, but also with my Rebbe (teacher), psychological mentor, companion, and trusted advisor.

In these decisive moments of my life I sensed his penetrating gaze visualizing the many difficulties and dangers confronting me in that faraway land out of his reach.

His refined lips tightened and as he tenderly held my hand he said, "My son, you are leaving for a strange land where rank materialism is the motivating force of the daily life. Success, of course, is important in everything we undertake and promote, but it is often of temporary duration. Granted that it may even prove enduring, it does not, as a rule, assure a life of real happiness and contentment."

I noted tears forming on his saddened eyes, and after some brief seconds of silence he continued.

"My son, in your young life you have by the Grace of the

Almighty triumphed over the lurking angel of death in a daring challenge of will power and sheer courage.

"You must forever remember that this priceless gift of life could not be repaid in any way to a compassionate creator who is responsible for preserving it for you.

"In the prestigious Yeshivahs you have been privileged to study in, you have been instilled with the untold spiritual values whose grandeur inflames a person's spark of godliness into a lighted torch of heavenly glory."

Father wiped off a tear from his flushed face and sent my rampaging emotions into a turbulent storm.

For it was once a year, at Yom Kipur Eve (Day of Atonement) supper, at its conclusion, that my father would gaze intently on the gathered family and, bursting out in a brief crying spell, would say, "Tate in Himmel (God in heaven), may none of us be missing in the year to come."

He then continued his discourse stating, "In the cavalcade of millenniums it was the devotional dedication to the creator and the Torah (Bible) that made it possible for our ancestors to survive the untold catastrophes and seemingly insurmountable, perilous dangers threatening us at every step of our unchartered journey."

Placing his hand on my shoulder tenderly as when we so pleasantly strolled the scenic pathways of the pine forest in leisure summer days, he said, "In your new homeland, life may be beset with unforeseen problems and difficulties, and often in trying times like that, one is prompted to part first with spiritual values to ease the prevailing burdens.

"In such decisive moments, remember my son, G'd saved you from the depth of grave to restore you with the priceless gift of life.

"The most plausible repayment to a gracious Almighty is to uphold the tenets and traditions inherited from posterity.

"For thousands of years countless generations have made the supreme sacrifice to preserve its heritage.

"I pray and hope, my son, that you too form an unbreakable link in that glorious chain for your children in days to come, to preserve the cherished treasure in an eternal bond with the universal creator."

Saying what was important to be said at such a telling moment, my father looked at his watch, so he would not miss the train's departure time back to Grodno, and embraced me in a last goodbye.

A bursting flow of tears broke the spell of my restrained emotions, but I soon calmed myself to state, "Father, I shall forever carry proudly the emblem of our untold traditions which I was so privileged to inherit.

"I shall gloriously treasure the devotional sacredness you so diligently instilled in me and the Yeshivahs that so inspired me."

With a parting kiss that forever seared the depth of my soul, my father left, turning to get a last look at me as he rounded the street corner on the way to the train.

As evening shadows deepened, the agent led us to a stable where a conestoga-type wagon padded with freshly cut hay was waiting for us to get in.

An elderly Mushic (farmer) and a younger one that seemed like his son vigilantly looked around outside and decided to wait.

About a half an hour later they peered again at the nearby lifeless street and thought it safe to start on our way.

Some miles away we passed a Dorf (farmer village) and were pelted with stones from both sides of the graveled roadway. I later learned the stones were thrown by rivals in border smuggling.

The drivers sent the two horses into a gallop that bounced us crazily all around the seatless wagon.

A few stones found their mark on a boy and girl, but luckily they resulted only in glancing blows.

About eleven o'clock the wagon entered a grain storage barn where we got out and waited long past midnight, walking then the dangerous miles leading to the perilous border crossing into Germany.

The young Mushic (farmer) gave us quiet instructions on how to follow him. Vigilantly he watched for border patrols, and when he expertly spotted some, we lay down flat in cornfields now at their full height.

Besides some clothes and food, I carried two goose-feather pillows, which my mother thought were non-existent in the United States, but soon I realized that holding on to them could prove catastrophic.

It was long past midnight when orders came to flop down in the cornfields, lay still, keep silent, and not make any disturbances since a Cossack cavalry unit was roaming the region.

It was not easy to lay still without moving as swarms of giant mosquitos mercilessly stung us with vengeance.

But I soon forgot about such nonsense when the hoofs of a Siberian Cossack steed stumbled on my bulky pillows, nearly striking my weary head.

Fearfully I realized that a mere feather pillow could have meant the end of it all if not for the fact that the stride of the speeding horse had obliterated such a flimsy object.

Undoubtedly I now reasoned that the timely Chofetz Chaim Brocho had been my savior.

It was nearly daybreak when we began our fateful walk to the German border, and we soon reached it at a point where the agent paid the two guarding soldiers for every person being smuggled out.

In order not to make telltale footprints on the ground, the soldiers arched their bodies over a narrow ravine and we passed over their backs across to the German border.

As if demons had been chasing us, we began running as fast as our mosquito-bitten feet would permit.

II

On the Way to the United States

With a feeling of tremendous relief we were led to a railroad station in a small German village where we washed, rested and left that very evening for the port city of Hamburg.

Early the following morning we arrived in that sprawling busy harbor where at one of the docks we boarded the slow-going but sturdy ship Batavia.

For nearly two weeks we made our way across the erratic Atlantic, sometimes calm and serene, at other times spitefully stormy.

Alone with myself, so naive and trustful, I soon discovered that the little I had with me was in time partly stolen. Even my Talis and Tefillin (religious objects) I found missing one day, but I somehow had sense enough to be watchful of the few silver rubles that the thieves missed in the early stages of plundering.

Like all things good or bad, sooner or later it was bound to change and soon, after nearly two weeks, the Atlantic crossing came to an end.

On a misty steaming August morning the outmoded but sturdy

Batavia cautiously navigated its bulky frame up the busy New York Harbor with an amalgamation of many nationalities and races forming so vividly the melting pot that made up the incomparable America.

Crowding the starboard side, the multi-national passengers riveted their gaze on the panoramic shoreline.

Like myself, they now envisioned their dreams, hopes and aspirations so clearly within their grasp.

Soon I heard the exciting chant, "Here she is! Here she is!" I too ran to a vantage point, and there loomed proudly in the hazy horizon the magnificent view of the stately Statue of Liberty.

Fascinated, I saw the grand regal lady with the seven-point crown gallantly holding high in her graceful arm a beacon of light.

Truly an eternal message of hope and promise for a suffering humanity to have trust and faith for better times to come.

At that time I had no inkling of what Emma Lazarus had inscribed on the glorious plaque, but even then, without yet making a single step on the treasured ground of the United States, I instinctively felt the meaning of those immortal words: Yes, give me your poor, your tired, your needy, downtroddenand wretched, yes and the homeless. I lift my lamp beside the golden door.

At that, one of the most inspiring moments in my life, I felt as though I owned the world.

And though I had but a dollar or maybe two to spare, I had a song in my heart and a divine melody in my soul that the treasured glory of Freedom and Liberty was here for humanity to cherish and embrace.

Gently the bulky Batavia glided into its docking position and everyone was finally ferried to Ellis Island, known to so many as the isle of tears, to those unfortunate thousands who could not be admitted to America.

Somehow no relative awaited me and I too had many anxious hours troubling me.

I watched thousands going on their way while I was yet unable to answer many questions since the emigration officials found my answers quite insufficient.

It was late in the day when I was informed that my uncle had called and all was cleared for me to board a train leaving for the Steel City which I would call my home for more than two years.

The first inkling that I had to beware of benevolent gift-givers was when I had settled down on the train and an authorized railroad vender offered some candy to any person willing to accept it.

I thought that this was the way a newly arrived immigrant was being welcomed. I was indeed hungry and this was just what I truly appreciated.

About five minutes later he made the rounds to collect either the candy or payment for it.

Not being able to speak English, I at first didn't understand what was going on, until a person from a nearby seat explained to me the situation in Yiddish.

It was then that I parted with my precious silver ruble, getting some change in return.

I arrived in McKees Rocks, a community across the river from Pittsburgh, where my Uncles Abraham and Meyer Silverman operated general men's clothing stores.

Uncle Meyer had a large family whose elder children helped in the business.

Uncle Abraham, who had two daughters and a son, employed a steady clerk with an extra on Saturdays and pre-holidays as he had a more extensive business.

For two weeks I resided in his home and I made myself quite useful in helping out in the store.

A large part of the clientele were Hungarian immigrants and my Uncle Abraham informed me that, as much as he would like to employ me, he must have a clerk who knew the Hungarian language.

Children of Fannie and Ely, in 1934. From left to right: Roland, Meta (holding Cleo), Myron, and Marquita.

The family of Ely's parents in 1902. Ely is seated in front row, left.

Fannie's mother, as a bride in Europe.

Children of Fannie and Ely, at early school age. From left to right: Marquita, Myron, Cleo, Meta, Roland.

I then moved to Pittsburgh and started on my own the best way I could.

Having no profession I first tried peddling and unfortunately, on bad advice, I began selling table oil cloth, the standard table cover used by miners.

Early one morning I went with the train to a mining village of "Moonron" many miles from Pittsburgh.

Unfortunately I did not make one sale all day, and with one single nickel left in my pocket and no return train ticket I decided to begin walking home.

But nagging hunger was sapping my strength and the heavy rolls of oil cloth rubbing my shoulders aggravated the situation.

At the outskirts of the village I noted an Italian woman placing freshly baked bread on her window sills, and nearby in a garden plot there were ripening tomatoes on the vine.

I pointed a finger to my mouth indicating I was hungry and then, pointing to the bread and tomatoes, I held up my precious nickel as a means of payment.

She smiled and sliced a large chunk of bread and then gave me a luscious tomato, and apologetically I gave her the meager payment in return.

Now sixty-five years later, I consider that meal the most elaborate banquet I ever was privileged to partake in.

Even now I can distinctly sense how, at every incisive bite, the godsent nourishment ingressed itself in my life's bloodstream.

It tingled my nerves with every body organ sending a message of revival.

The sun began sinking in the panoramic setting of the Allegheny mountain range when I started with new vigor down its wooded trails on my five-mile walk to Pittsburgh.

I did not feel any shoulder pain or fatigue from a wasted day, and somehow I just felt I had to keep on singing.

I sang beautiful high holiday hymns, Hebrew songs by the Poet Laureate Nachman Bialik and other songs I knew well, even some Russian songs by Lermontov and Pushkin.

A cool September breeze began to chill me as evening shadows quickly cooled the warmth of a sunny day and I was glad to get home for a weary deserving rest.

Later that evening I asked my landlady to loan me a quarter, with which I went down to a corner lunchroom where I had a tasty fifteen-cent meal, with ten cents left for the next day's breakfast.

For more than two years I struggled for a mere daily subsistence, since the economic conditions were somehow unfavorable and changing jobs left me without any outlook for future progress.

In those trying years I very often found solace and contentment in visiting synagogues and getting absorbed in Talmudic studies, which were so deeply ingrained in my heart and soul.

In such grand moments I melodiously recited the Talmudic discourse as if sailing away in heavenly splendor.

It brought back the memory of my unforgettable years in the Yeshivahs when, at an age of pure idealism, I felt keenly the sanctified touch of the heavenly creator.

Vividly I envisioned my fellow students, many so devoid of the very necessities of life, yet so sincere and devoted and united with me in a divine bond of untold faithfulness. Truly no worldly richness could have compensated for our treasured spiritual glory.

I often noted many people observing my devotional studies. They probably wondered how long such idealism could survive in this land of pragmatic actions.

My boarding house was what was referred to as a cold-water apartment where on winter nights the numbing cold was at times unbearable.

I found some relief when, at times, I would go to a nickelodeon where, for five or ten cents, I could enjoy a movie and the pleasing piano playing by an enthusiastic musician.

And what was most important, a comfortable seat in a warm place, so cozy and content.

THE ARRIVAL OF MY PARENTS

King David in one of his most inspiring psalms states that if one wants to visualize the rhyme, reason and purpose of life, one could easily determine it from the intricate pattern of his personal life.

That came to my mind when I pondered the miraculous departure of my parents and family for the United States during the ominous war year of 1917.

Grodno was then occupied by the German army with General Hindenburg, the supreme army commander, making his headquarters in the Governor's Palace on Sodowa Street.

All through that fateful year, not a single Jewish family was permitted to emigrate from Grodno to any other state.

Then one day my father recalled an incident that motivated him to seemingly try the impossible.

The telling episode had taken place in 1905 when the prestigious Grodno yeshivah was in danger of being closed.

As was the rule, such a decision had to be determined at a meeting where two delegates each from the forty-one synagogues would elect to vote on it. (As with United States Senators, two of which are elected from each state, large or small, the same was true with the synagogue delegates.)

At that meeting it was decided that there was no way the community could adequately finance the yeshivah and it had to be closed.

My father, as the delegate of the Klaus Synagogue, was the last speaker and, in a satirical vein, pointed to several millionaires present and asked them, "When your alloted lifetime span on earth terminates and you are asked for the heavenly record why you voted to abandon the Yeshivah, you will say because we were short of funds."

He then pointed to those prominent delegates and said, "You, Shereshewsky, you, Bame Frumkin, you, Ashkenazy, you, Katznelenson, you, Risota, and so on, you could not afford to contribute a little more to its required maintenance." Following his speech, another vote was taken where it was determined to preserve the yeshivah in its full, prestigious glory.

In Grodno there lived a remarkable person who devoted his entire life to alleviate the sufferings of the needy and those requiring assistance in any way to make life easier.

His name was "Reb Nochum," with an added tribute, "the saint."

Some days after my father's efforts resulted in that favorable vote to keep up the Yeshivah, the saintly Reb Nochum came to my mother's herring store and said, "Alte" (Alte being my mother, Rachel's, nickname), "just as Chatzkel (my father's nickname) saved the Yeshivah, G'd will save his life in time of danger."

Inspired by the promise and the cherished prediction of "Reb Nochum, the saint," my father courageously went one blustery winter day to the Governor's palace, and to the astonishment of the watchful sentries he asked to see the General in charge.

Stunned in sheer disbelief at the sight of an elderly, bearded Jew wanting to meet with a commanding German General, the sentry gave him a positive "No" for an answer.

But when my father assured him that the General will be pleased to hear what he had to say, the sentry relayed the message to the proper officials and, to his astonishment, the General agreed to meet him.

My father, by the grace of God, must have made a favorable impression on the high-ranking officer, who gave him right then a permit to leave with his family for the United States.

For the nearly twenty thousand Jewish people of Grodno, this sounded like a fanciful fable in an illusionary dream, and on the day my parents departed from Grodno thousands went to the railroad station to actually see if this miracle was truly taking place.

My father's efforts did not come any too soon, for shortly thereafter the German Government decreed unrestricted submarine warfare and no ships would sail anymore to the United States.

MY RETURN TO NEW YORK

A few weeks after their arrival in New York, I left Pittsburgh to join and live with them.

On my way to New York, I recalled the tearful parting with my family in 1914 which seemed then as if it was forever.

Surely I thought the spiritual vision of such saintly men like the Chofetz Chaim and Reb Nochum, the Saint, are beyond ordinary mortals to envision and understand.

With my parents arrived a younger brother and two unmarried sisters, and how to get organized economically was quite an urgent problem to solve.

I had already begun to master the English language and could now, to some extent, take care of my personal needs, but I was unable to be of any worthwhile help to the family.

But as water always finds its proper level, the economic conditions began to stabilize themselves with the passing of time.

My father, who would not accept a paid Rabbinical position as a means of livelihood, accepted one at the Marcy Avenue Synagogue in Brooklyn, for he now felt it was justified under the prevailing conditions of economic stress.

My sisters and brother also managed to find occasional employment, but my prospective outlook for a fundamental economic base was not at all encouraging.

In a way I felt a sense of inferiority, because, being almost three years in the States, I had nothing to show for it.

Like a transplanted tree in an unsuitable environment, I could adjust myself neither economically or spiritually although the opportunities were truly so readily available.

My wonderful, understanding mother said very little, but in the warmth of her benevolent and mellow gaze, she expressed the perplexity of my uncomfortable situation.

As to my father, my lack of any material progress was no surprise, for his perceptive, logical mind had determined long ago that a Rabbinical mission was what I was meant to have and any other vocation was to be a hit-or-miss proposition.

III

The Fateful Year of 1920

In Brooklyn, New York resided a family friend of long standing: Mr. Schwartz. He was also a close friend to a family by the name of Cohen who resided in Mount Carmel, Pennsylvania.

One day when I arrived home after my day's clerking in a wholesale general dry goods store, I found him visiting us.

His well-balanced body was equally moderated by a rhythmical, expressive and unhurried way of conversing.

That evening he spoke to me in a sincere and fatherly manner, the essence of which was that he knew a girl who was a real treasure and that we could form a marital union which would be a divine blessing to us and an envy for people to see.

Mr. Schwartz left home very encouraged and rightly so, for one unruly winter day I decided to go up to meet the girl, and our blissful marital union proved to be the Almighty's eternal gift, almost as priceless as life itself.

Leaving New York on the Lehigh Valley Railroad, the towering steam engine had it all its own way until in the dead of that foggy winter night it reached the steep upgrade of little Mahanoy Mountain.

It began sliding resoundingly on the churning turns of the slippery rails.

Climbing ever higher, its spinning wheels raced furiously around themselves, while lavas of spewing, live steam hissed frantically, its vaporous spray freezing instantly at the numbing touch of the mountain air.

The fireman must have undoubtedly doubled his efforts to feed the monster boiler as the raw bituminous coal sent belching clouds of acrid smoke rolling in endless waves.

I watched through the steamed window panes, the burning embers and glowing cinders whirling furiously in a raging furor of maddening defiance.

The three dimly lighted wooden coaches with trailing caboose creaked and groaned as the frustrated engine started and stopped.

Continually the captive cars resounded defiantly, clashing noisily against the steel couplings binding them together.

At times the engine backed away, only to furiously make a new effort, and with an angry lurch forward it sent the train into a convulsive tremor.

In the far distance loomed burning coal banks, their sulphuric greenish blue flame reflecting eerily in the engulfing mountain clouds.

I was then alone, lonely, insecure in my job and facing an uncertain tomorrow when the train made its last stop at the dimly gaslighted Mount Carmel station.

As if in triumph from its remarkable accomplishments, the train backed away noisily to the railroad yards, with bells merrily ringing and whistles madly blaring.

Carefully I crossed in the stark, foggy darkness over the multiple tracks leading to a deserted, hilly road, heading to the coal-mining town of Mount Carmel.

Envisioning now that fateful winter day on my way to meeting my lifetime partner, I so inspiringly remember the providential designs that mold a person's life.

PERILOUS COURTSHIP DAYS AHEAD

Fannie, at the age of nineteen, was the virtual manager of her father's clothing and furniture store, but it was far from the real ambition she had dreamed about ever since childhood.

Stricken with scarlet fever at the age of five, Fannie suffered grieviously with a notable hearing loss.

She nevertheless excelled in her schooling despite this handicap.

Though tormented by school pupils and others due to her hearing loss, Fannie endured it with a fortitude that was truly divine.

Once, while she was attending the sixth grade, the teacher called for volunteers to recite Lincoln's Gettysburg Address. The only student to respond was Fannie, who narrated the speech in a manner that aroused tremendous admiration.

Even while in the elementary school, Fannie helped her father in his struggling business.

Her indispensable presence resulted in her inability to continue with a high school education, which remained a painfully illusive dream.

Fannie had an inherited urge and a talent for fashion designing, and also a keen sense of music.

All those facts I learned later as we began our courtship, and it made me wonder then if we were compatible for a happy marital union.

I meditated the barriers that divided us.

Fannie loved music while I had no inkling of its potential values.

She had inherited a deep-felt sense of artistic virtues, which I lacked.

Fannie's pragmatic mentality was self-evident in the management of her father's business and in making facts count, while I was an addicted spiritual dreamer.

Fannie had mastered in bookkeeping while I had no profession of any kind.

Her father's business required experience and capital, and in that respect I surely could not be helpful.

At our fateful first get-together I was overwhelmed by such a talented, warm-hearted, feminine personality, which was so truly rare.

But, I thought, though Fannie had the various qualities to make me happy, could I in return bring contentment and sunshine to her life?

That was a question that constantly beguiled my mind, yet in the span of two days of getting acquainted, the invisible threads of common values and understanding weaved a magic bond of friendship.

How heartening it was to have the Cohens ask me to remain another day if possible, which I gladly did.

That day also had its unpleasantness for me, as some Jewish neighbors paid an unexpected evening visit to the Cohens.

Mount Carmel in the year of 1919 had two Jewish shoemakers, two tailors, three junk dealers, three professionals and the others in retail business.

The two visiting women were from the elite, the more prominent in the community.

One was a very attractive middle-aged woman, the other one in contrast a real mieskeit (ugly). Fannie happened to play on the piano "Let me call you sweetheart, I'm in love with you." Her other song was "I love you not only a day, not a year, but always."

I was upstairs when I heard the mieskeit say, "Fannie, is this an accolade to a lover?"

At that time I did not know what the meaning was of the word accolade, and that was what seemed to have reduced my importance with them.

It was an era when new immigrants arrived in a constant flow, and those already Americanized to a certain degree looked askance at the newcomers, referring to them as "greenies" or "greenhorns."

In such a way they felt that it enhanced their own importance in so-called intelligence.

Fannie smiled when I came downstairs to the living room and she introduced me to the unexpected guests.

I too smiled somewhat benignly as I felt myself scrutinized from the top of the head to the style of my shoes.

I sat down comfortably getting in some meaningless conversation, and once in a while the visiting women would gaze at each other expressing in their pantomimed reactions their evaluation of me.

It was my last evening and I would have appreciated spending the time with Fannie, something they seemingly did not realize.

In my several later visits this situation seemed to repeat itself, and I learned that I didn't pass their tests at any time at all.

Very devotedly and earnestly some women would state that I seemed to be a very nice boy, polite and sensible, but not for Fannie.

"She is an Americanized girl and he is a greenhorn. He should have managed to learn English much better, his dialect, to say the least, is awful," someone would say and then add, "I better keep quiet, say nothing."

"What do you mean say nothing!" exclaimed another. "We don't want to hurt the poor boy, but it's Fannie's future at stake, it's our duty as friends to speak honestly and frankly our candid opinion."

Though I did not realize the extent of their deliberations, I instinctively felt that my position was constantly deteriorating.

I recalled an old Jewish saying: "A Katz can eich kalie machen" (even a cat could do utmost damage)."

That Wednesday I was nevertheless inspired by the thought that love and common understanding could overcome any of life's difficulties and I was in an elated mood.

Before checking out of the marble-hall hotel I went down to the basement barber shop where Erick Bates, the master barber, suggested a massage and shampoo.

"Why?" I asked him. "You noticed any dandruff?" "Oh no! No way! None of it," he apologized. "Only, I know it is very refreshing and it does make a difference, especially when one is to meet a girl friend."

I smilingly agreed that on such a special occasion he was a hundred-percent right.

I went to the dining room for breakfast and the amiable waitress said, "I know, no ham and eggs, just eggs on toast. I often have such religious Jewish people who observe the law," she added.

About eleven o'clock I went to bid farewell to the Cohens, thanking them for their most wonderful hospitality, with Fannie volunteering to accompany me to the railroad station, the train leaving shortly for New York.

I had no way at that time of knowing what were Fannie's thoughts and feelings about me, but when I bid her goodbye, I felt in her warm handshake and pleasant smile the inception of a friendship that would not so easily be uprooted.

But circumstances and time have their own mystical way of circumventing a person's designs and plans.

A prolonged strike in the Mount Carmel region was playing devastating havoc with the surrounding economy.

The Cohens' business, especially in furniture, was largely on credit.

Outstanding bills remained unpaid and bankers were reluctant to make loans in these unpredictable situations.

There was a large mortgage on their building with several payments of interest due (there is a well-known Talmudic quotation: When there is no wheat in the receptacle, there is misunderstandings in the household).

The same held true in the Cohen family, it was economics that counted most now.

During my several visits, we learned more and more to understand each other affectionately, but it wasn't binding enough to withstand the grinding stress of life's burdensome tensions.

Not being near each other to strengthen the strands that began to entwine our souls also complicated matters and I keenly realized that where there is no progress there is gradual disintegration.

One thing was now most important and that was proving to Fannie and her parents my ability for spectacular advancement, and at the time, the outlook was actually non-existent.

That is, for a mortal it was a virtual impossibility, but then wasn't I fortunate to receive the Chofetz Chaim's brocho (blessings)!

So the miracle that I could not have visualized in my wildest dreams came my way at a time that was so fatefully telling.

I was clerking at that time for a very progressive businessman named M.L. Pollard. He operated the Washington Mills, a wholesale dry goods firm occupying a multi-floored building at 593 Broadway.

The firm employed thirty-four people, more than half of them assigned to gathering together the incoming orders arriving daily.

I observed that there was much inefficiency and time loss in the system they worked by.

Once in a while I would suggest to the manager, Mr. Rosenberg, that much improvement could be made saving time and cost.

This Mr. Rosenberg was a college graduate with a very impressive personality.

Every time I would humbly make one of those suggestions, he scratched the side of his head and wondered why no one ever thought of it before.

Somehow I thought nothing of it and did not realize that Mr. Rosenbert would have the honesty to relate my suggestions with praise to Mr. Pollard.

During those months considerable shortages were discovered in the stock inventory, and I once heard the manager and assistant manager discuss it.

I long ago realized the vulnerability to pilfering and theft in that loosely operating system, and it was just a matter of common sense and logic to plug those loopholes.

Again I conveyed my ideas to Mr. Rosenberg, who again scratched his head, only more than ever.

One day Mr. M.L. Pollard went down in the basement where I sorted incoming orders and said, "Ely, I admire the many suggestions that you made, and I want you to know that I really appreciate it."

Mr. Pollard was tall, somewhat portly, resembling Chief United States Supreme Court Justice Howard Taft. He had a radiant, pinkish-colored face, but was very intensely dynamic. I shook his hand most heartily and I assured him that my Talmudic education was invaluable to me in utilizing my abilities and sense of dedication for those who entrusted me with their problems.

It was at that very time that Mrs. Rosenberg's parents opened a department store in Atlanta, Georgia and placed Mr. Rosenberg in full charge of it.

It also happened that the assistant manager, Mr. Berger, moved with his family to Los Angeles, California with his parent preceding him.

Before they left, Mr. Pollard asked their advice about the most suitable person to be entrusted with the manager's position, and they both recommended me.

One glorious day in a sunny April as I prepared to leave from work, Mr. Pollard came over to me and shocked me by handing over to me the keys to the business.

Now more serious than usual he said, "I am taking a most daring step. I am entrusting you with the responsibility of supervising the business.

"From now on, you are in charge as a manager. If you do what is right there is a great future awaiting you.

"You will advance with my success, and the prospects are tremendous." he added.

If there was ever a moment in my life when I actually saw the Almighty in his full glory, it was now.

I was in a trance, I tightly held Mr. Pollard's hand in my gripping palm, speechless for a while, and finally said, "Mr. Pollard, I will do my most dedicated best, and it will more than justify your expectations."

When I brought home this unbelievable news, there was an acclamation of sheer joy, tears, laughter and smiles, mingling in a symphony of raptured ecstasy.

My mother softly cried, shedding tears of joy, while my father quoted the Bible stating, "Etzba Elohim hu (it is the hand of G'd)."

This indeed called for some form of jubilation and we began it with our evening meal.

My older sister went down to the corner grocery store, got some white fish, real farmer's cream cheese, fresh-baked rolls and bagels, and some fruitcake for dessert.

Mother changed tablecloths, bringing out a bottle of carmel wine from which we toasted for many more blessings to come.

Even before we sat down to eat, I went to a drugstore a few blocks away on Myrtle Avenue and called Fannie to tell her of the miraculous happenings.

She was truly amazed and wanted to be certain if I hadn't drifted into a temporary delusion.

I admitted that I had to pinch myself frequently to make certain it was not a dream.

The drugstore building trembled violently every time a Myrtle Avenue elevated train passed. There was also quite a bit of static in the phone so our conversation was brief.

But even at that, I sensed her elation at such a giant step forward in my life, and of course, in a way equally for her.

About a week later Mr. Cohen came to New York, seemingly on business, but I suspected more to learn if what I had told them had really materialized.

The Black Diamond express train starting its run in Buffalo arrived in New Jersey early morning, and after crossing from its

New Jersey terminal by ferry it was still not quite opening hours for business establishments.

The first thing on Mr. Cohen's agenda was to head for 593 Broadway, the Washington Mills.

Arriving there, he saw a few dozen people waiting at the door. He went over to ask what were they waiting for.

"There is a short delay on the incoming subway from Brooklyn and our manager is late opening the business," he was told.

"Who is your manager?" he inquired.

"A Mr. Ely Moskowitz, a fine young man who recently advanced as manager," he was told.

That day he took an early train back to Mount Carmel and elatedly told his family they didn't realize the extent of my potential qualifications.

This miraculous event, whose fantastic implications bordered on the bizarre, was the magical wand that sealed our marital union on a long, difficult and dangerous journey, yet one which was so blissful and meaningful.

During the first week in May, Mr. Pollard granted me a week's vacation with pay and I went up to Mount Carmel to enjoy my companionship with Fannie.

I noticed that Fannie's parents were somewhat upset and nervous, and one time as we went up Meriam Mountain to taste some of the pure spring water, Fannie jokingly told me that her parents were worried that conscienceless troublemakers might yet succeed in delaying or thwarting our marriage.

"Are you serious?" I asked her, sealing it with a kiss in our lonely mountain stroll.

"You don't know smalltown gossip and its evil designs," she replied.

And the saying came to my mind again: "A katz (cat) could also do irreversible damage."

Those turbulent months that in a way most fantastic fiction paled against were too important to gamble with, and on a rainy

May day we arranged a civil wedding, with our religious nuptials to take place on June 6th.

In a row of old wooden houses near the corner of Fourth and Oak Streets there was the one-room office of Squire King.

In the small, low-ceilinged room a coal-burning heater occupied its center where Fluffy, a watchful dog, keenly scrutinized the incoming clientele.

If it was a criminal hearing, he would alertly arise as if the policeman's presence was not enough to protect the judicial squire.

And he was helpless indeed, Squire King being of medium height but with a tremendous width to span. He conducted his judicial statutory decisions from a spacious swivel chair he barely fitted into.

With no back window for ventilation and an unusual low ceiling to boot, its stifling air was, to say the least, quite uncomfortable.

Fortunately the door was partly open and Squire King executed all formalities in a matter of about ten minutes' time.

Without getting off the swivel chair, his birdlike face lighted up in a pleasing smile as he congratulated us for a life of health and happiness.

As Mr. Cohen paid him the legal fees, he quietly told him that the ceremony was not for publication or, for that matter, for anyone's knowledge outside the immediate family.

"You should know me better than that, Nathan (Cohen's first name)."

Somehow we could not realize then the full impact as to what had transpired.

In a mere few minutes we had legally bound our lives together, but the ease and simplicity of its performance robbed us of the glory which such a momentous occasion is meant to have.

But the knowledge that our real nuptial union would take place on June 6th compensated greatly for this shortcoming.

For nearly a month before the religious wedding we were legally man and wife, residing together in the same home.

It was a strange setup, we were religious to the point where we aimed to preserve the Biblical laws, but since we were human, it required much willpower and courage to suppress temptation.

Every morning we would kid each other, "Where were you? Someone was hiding."

The Cohens had an abiding faith in our fidelity while we were hoping that we didn't stumble into nature's tantalizing bewitchments.

Time does indeed pass quickly and on June 6th the providential marital union came our way.

My father was then Rabbi in the Marcy Avenue Synagogue, Brooklyn, but the wedding was performed at the Willoughby Avenue Shull (Synagogue), which had a spacious social hall with all the facilities required for such an auspicious occasion.

Rabbi Inzelbook, its spiritual leader, was the one who performed the ceremony, but five other regional Rabbis participated to make it an outstanding affair.

My mother-in-law, Nahama, who always dreamed of being part of a Rabbinical family, was now walking on air as Rabbis and Rebetzins (Rabbis' wives) kept on greeting her with countless Mazoltovs (good luck).

Fannie and I had special reason to smile, for we had stood the test of temptation for so many weeks and our conscience was clear amidst this venerable assembly steeped in religious traditions and laws.

OUR HONEYMOON WEEK

Monday morning the Cohens returned to Mount Carmel while Fannie and I paid an overdue visit to Mr. Pollard at the Washington Mills, where he greeted us most enthusiastically now, with a hearty well-wishing and cordial Mazoltov.

"To be candid, Mr. Pollard, said Fannie, "what made you appoint a manager who not only did not possess a college education, but not even an elementary school education?"

Mr. Pollard smiled with the most affectionate grin I had ever seen from him and then said seriously, "Mrs. Moskowitz, I was born in the United States, became an orphan at seven when my father passed away, and I was fortunate to conclude the fifth grade when I went out to get any work helping my mother and the four other younger children.

"I bypassed many who had education and worldly means, until today I am considered one of the most progressive businessmen in our trading line.

"To a large extent it was due to the fact that I have a keen sense of understanding of human nature and the intrinsic values of gifted individuals.

"During Mr. Moskowitz's eight months' employment, I was convinced that he is a rare, dedicated personality possessing unadulterated common sense and logic, and that is the reason why college degrees are at times less important than superb individual qualifications," he stated.

We parted with most cordial thanks since, though Mr. Pollard didn't realize it, his action of naming me manager may have been mostly responsible for our marital union.

Honeymooning in New York, Fannie had her mind set on touring the fascinating amalgamation of the East Side, and on Tuesday morning it was the first thing on our schedule.

We began our walking circuit on East Broadway near the Jewish Daily Forward Building and by chance went in a small, tidy restaurant to have breakfast.

The restaurant was located a few stairs below the street level, it had about ten tables, most of them with four seats to a table, more than half of them now occupied.

At many of them lively conversations were taking place, all of them in "Yiddish."

Next to where we sat, a young, tall, dark-complected man with dreamful brown eyes was reciting a handwritten poem to a middle-aged thoughtful person who, with eyes half-closed, listened intently to evaluate its merits.

At another table I overheard a union organizer complaining about a Communist plot to take control of a garment local.

The waiter arrived to take our order with the owner busy in the kitchen preparing the meals.

We were the only ones that spoke English and it probably drew the attention of the owner, who shortly passed our table with a hearty good morning and then went back.

Something must have struck a resounding chord in the back of his mind for, soon after, he casually ventured past us giving me a scrutinizing side glance.

I thought nothing of it until he came back to ask me if I was born in Grodno.

"You must be a magician," I said, "you guessed right, Grodno is my birthplace."

"Are you Reb Chatzkel's son," he inquired excitedly.

"That's right," I said, "and may I know who you are?"

"You sure will be surprised to know. I am Bernard Tropp, the one who picked you up when the team of horses ran over you.

"It was I who got a Droshky (a carriage) to rush you to the Hekdesh (hospital). Had there been any delay, you would have bled to death."

We embraced each other with Fannie looking on in disbelief at this nostalgic scene, and we reminisced about those memorable days from the distant past.

Soon everyone in the restaurant had learned of this amazing reunion that bordered on make-believe fiction.

The poet said it would make a good theme for a poem and Mr. Tropp promised him a free full-course dinner when he completed it.

When we left, Mr. Tropp promised to get in touch with us and my parents, and we promised to visit him whenever we got to New York.

What a providential beginning for a honeymoon on this gorgeous day in June. It surely foretells good tidings to come, I ventured to predict.

"Halwai (may it prove true)," stated Fannie, to whom this fantastic scenario seemed like a magical scene.

TOURING THE EAST SIDE

Fannie came with her parents to Mount Carmel at the age of four and, with the exception of one visit on Bushwick Avenue in Brooklyn, she never returned to see the many interesting sights in that amalgamated metropolis.

I too had little opportunity to get acquainted with New York's East Side during my two years adjusting myself economically.

So now it was most timely for us to enjoy the interesting and exciting sights and events.

We went from East Broadway to Orchard, Eldridge, Suffolk and other surrounding streets, which was indeed quite an experience to behold.

The streets were lined up with endless rows of five- and six-story structures. Their uniform brick walls and windows entangled in a criss-cross web of overhanging fire escapes.

Many had entrances to basement store rooms with iron rails for stairs leading to the apartment hallways.

In the semi-darkened corridors there was a constant movement of people leaving or coming to or from the cold-water tenements and flats.

Beneath and near the stairs were entrances to narrow, small store rooms whose variety of articles sold were truly legendary.

On the sidewalk by the curb were carts, tables and stands selling anything from a spool of thread to a winter fur coat, and from ladies' corsets to men's suspenders. In fact, it was a department store in the making.

On the edge of the curb on the street came another line of

pushcarts that could be wheeled in or out with a similar endless assortment of items to beguile the imagination. Men's wear and ladies' garments were intermingled with cosmetics and footwear of all kinds and the competition was really keen.

In between were section upon section where the sale of food predominated.

Wide rounded barrels of Shmaltz Herring stood side by side with sour pickles and cucumbers, while basins had live fish that splashed fitfully to escape their entrapment.

There were sections predominating with religious articles, selling Mezuzos, silk and wool talaisim, prayer books and also books of Jewish and Hebrew writers, while next to them there was a rush to buy freshly baked bread, bagels, rolls, their invigorating aroma so notable.

With both sides of the streets' edges occupied, there was very little space left for traffic.

Old-fashioned wagons drawn by half-sleepy horses slowly made their way while the impatient drivers of automobiles frantically sounded their horns for them to move on.

By the sight of it the wagon drivers couldn't have cared less, seemingly leaving it to the discretion of their faithful steeds to decide when it was time and safe to get going.

On the overcrowded sidewalks the pushing and shoving was a condition everyone seemed to have gotten accustomed to.

At times a temporary fracas would suddenly erupt when two customers would hold onto a bargain item, each one claiming he or she had got a hold of it first.

I witnessed an amazing scene when a fashionably dressed aristocratic-looking lady, undoubtedly from a prestigious section of New York, held onto such a claimed bargain.

Arguing with her was a poorly dressed, middle-aged woman with faded bedroom slippers completing her mode of attire, contending that she would swear by the Holy Torah (Bible) that she had got a hold of it first.

From the assembling crowd, witnesses suddenly appeared to justify the poor woman's claims.

When the aristocratic woman left in disgust, I heard someone say, "Was deinkstu far asa chutzpo (what do you think of such arrogance), the richer they are, the more they want.

"The erd is tzu klein far zei (the earth is too small for them)."

As we kept strolling in this fantastic mercantile setup, we passed a stand where a tall, red-bearded man dressed in Semi-Rabbinical garb kept on arranging and rearranging his meager stock of men's socks, handkerchiefs, belts and other minor items.

The rearrangements did not seem to improve anything, but evidently making himself busy was a way to lessen his nervous tension from the lack of customers.

Further up the street we noted a mild-mannered person about the age of forty sadly watching a customer get ready to make a purchase, only to change his mind at the last minute. A little girl about seven years old standing near him curiously asked, "What happened, he did not buy?" To which he said somewhat impatiently, "My dear Esther, you always seem to ask such queer questions. How should I know what people decide to do, you think I am a prophet?"

Shortly after the man returned and said, "Mister, ich will doss Kaifen (I will buy it)."

The owner smiled showering him with thanks as he departed.

On the same stand Fannie spotted some colorful scarfs so she bought some. "I could sell it for twice its price in our Mount Carmel store," she whispered to me.

The owner again thanked her in profusion when she paid him.

As we left I noticed how he gave the little Esther some money telling her to hurry to give it to her mother. "She is waiting for it, be sure you don't lose it," he cautioned her.

Further up the street Fannie was fascinated by a display of ornamental jewelry, one dollar maximum price. She bought a cameo and asked the vivacious lady, "What happens to the long line of exposed stands and pushcarts in case of a sudden storm?"

The perplexed lady scratched her head as if to extract a proper answer from there and smilingly said, "Somehow we miraculously manage to survive."

We were fascinated and time went fast as we strolled leisurely the entwining streets of Ludlow, Suffolk, Rivington, Grand, Broom, Delancey and others, until we found ourselves on Division Street.

Suddenly we discovered that this part of the East Side truly belonged to the environments of Park or Fifth Avenue.

It seemed to specialize in ladies' fashionable and stylish clothes. Display after display in windows lured Fannie to admire their tastefulness. Since childhood, fashion designing had been her inborn trait and here too she would tell me how a little extra touch or change would add greatly to a garment's fashionable dimensions. Such classical designing was as baffling to me as the Chinese alphabet and all that remained for me to do now was to listen and say nothing.

A most dramatic window display of fabulous dresses featured shimmering Persian-designed materials, blending in a gorgeous array of sparkling hues.

At that point Fannie could not resist anymore the temptation of entering the store to explore its glamorous contents.

Well-dressed men waited on customers attentively and unhurriedly.

A meticulously attired manager with a pointed silk kerchief in his lapel pocket came over to ask if he could be of any service to us.

"No," said Fannie, "I truly have no particular item in mind but if I see something to my liking, I will call on you."

While making the rounds of that fabulous display of fashionable garments, Fannie said quietly to me, "With the miners in the Mount Carmel region working part time and at times also striking, it's even a sin thinking about buying such expensive clothes, but it is worthwhile to know how the other half of the world is living and spending."

When we left no one seemed to care whether we made any purchase or not.

Evidently it was a lucrative business where they did not depend on the day's receipts to cover outstanding checks arriving in the bank.

Like everything in life that is joyful and pleasant, the honeymoon week went fast. Indeed way too fast as we returned now to the grinding realities of our daily life.

But our arrival back in Mount Carmel wasn't without its exciting frivolities.

When the Lehigh Valley train came to its last stop at the dimly lighted Mount Carmel station in an early evening, Dominick McKenzie's five piece band awaited us.

Dominick was a miner at the Alaska colliery and he formed the musical band for extra earnings, but this performance was not for money as he was a devoted customer in my father-in-law's store.

Once he boasted, "What Nathan Cohen don't have, I order it to get later on."

Relatives and friends were also waiting there and together we marched in a festive parade down to a huge hall at the corner of Oak and Third Street, where we celebrated late into the night, eating, drinking and dancing to the lively tunes of our good friend McKenzie.

Indeed an unexpected treat, a real surprise party long to be remembered.

OPENING A STORE

A new leaf soon turned in our exciting young life, which in a way formed the fundamental basis of our economic direction in the decades to come.

On the corner of Shamokin and Independence Streets in Shamokin, a ladies' hat store went out of business and I ventured to open a family shoestore there.

The storeroom was only about sixty feet long and in a triangle form, but it had a high ceiling which I thought would make up in shelving space, with sliding ladders to reach the shoe contents.

Shamokin was at that time considered the business metropolis of the lower anthracite coal region, with no stores available to rent.

I seemed to be a man in a hurry and I chanced to rent it before someone else got it.

People who knew that I had no experience whatsoever in the footwear line ridiculed my senseless move as foolhardy, but I thought that nothing ventured is nothing gained, Fannie agreeing with me.

I was nevertheless truly amazed when my business proved an instant success.

Right across from my corner store, beyond an immense plaza, loomed the Eagle silk mill, a huge compound of six-story red-brick buildings erected on a multi-acre tract.

It employed at times more than two thousand women, and when pay day came, the plaza exit became an onrushing mass of thrilling humanity eager to spend their earnings on their and their families' needs.

Many of that hurrying mass would rush in my store and, when there remained standing room only, the overflow would leave for other shoestores to be served.

Complicating my shortage of space was the fact that fitting up a lady customer was indeed an intricate matter.

The most desirable style at that time was ladies' high shoes which almost reached the knees. Some were laced on hooks and no matter how fast it was done, it was tedious and time-absorbing.

But the real culprits were those that buttoned. One had to be an expert to perform that skillful task, especially on ankles that thickened abruptly so that laced shoes could be adjusted but not those that buttoned. And women with such a problem would often accuse the clerk of missing the button on purpose in order to feel their legs.

To me it now became a problem of too much prosperity and I often had to make special calls to Thomson and Crooker Shoe Company in Cincinnati, Ohio for rush-order shipments.

Within months Mr. Greaber, the president of the National Bank, noticed my success from which I had established an enviable bank record and placed a substantial credit at my disposal.

In fact, when several years later I bought a business building on the main street, I had no difficulty in financing it with a forty-thousand-dollar banking mortgage.

We resided the first year with my in-laws in a second floor, three-room, artistically furnished apartment, and on some tranquil evenings I could not help boasting to Fannie that I seemed to have acquired the King Midas touch.

Fannie knocked on wood, though she was not superstitious, and said, "Let's be thankful to a gracious almighty and, better yet, let's not brag about it."

But I could not help recalling that but three years ago, I was changing jobs, depending on others to provide me with a livelihood, with some considering it a great favor.

It was on one of those tumultuous, active days when Fannie learned that she was in the family way, and our joyful happiness was beyond words to describe.

In the tree-lined residential street in our Mount Carmel home, a towering age-old oak fronted our windows.

During spring, summer and part of autumn, the lush of its verdant greenery would persistently press against the house.

Its twigs and extended branches fingered their way into our open windows with a heavenly fragrance.

Fannie and I now looked at this inspiring scene and saw the blessed event to come and the Divine joy it would bring with it.

Once a sudden summer storm sent the majestic tree into a raging upheaval. It seemed to be nature's way of using fury and raging tempest in order to calm its temper.

Fannie benignly smiled and jestingly said, "I wonder what are our family records concerning our tempers."

"I guess we all possess a fair share to balance it out," I suggested.

When the storm finally subsided Fannie philosophically stated, "Evidently to appreciate the good, one must endure the qualms of passing storms."

What was supposed to be a secret, at least for a while, soon became common knowledge.

I once overheard a neighbor asking a friend if she heard the latest news. "Oh that! I knew it before you. Mrs. Moleski told me that a week ago."

After a while some would boldly ask, "Fannie, tell me, is that true what I heard about you?" To which Fannie would say, "Rumors sometimes happen to justify themselves."

On some restless nights Fannie would at times awaken me to describe the sensuous palpitations of the forming child and to perceive so thrillingly the pulsating throbs of generating life in the wondrous process of creation.

Thoughtfully I would envision that heavenly designed magic of a tiny form now so fervidly and instinctively probing endlessly to expand its space, find nourishment and a way to complete its providential perfection.

Some inspiring evenings Fannie would go down to the living room and pliantly manipulate her sensitive fingers on the piano to express her inspired mood in tuneful songs, her dreamful hopes and new-born aspirations.

That year on Yom Kippur (day of atonement) her mother, Nahama, left home earlier than usual and was the first to arrive on the Synagogue balcony reserved for women.

There she sat on the front seat by the railing, her beautiful, mellow brown eyes visualizing the holy ark with the Torah (Bible) scrolls always within sight.

It was nearly nine o'clock in the morning when the all-day-long services began and Nahama remained standing in the creator's respect.

Not once did she sit down until the day of atonement concluded shortly after sunset.

Attired in a gleaming white, brocaded silk dress with high-heel white pumps to match, Nahama did not mind the day's fasting, fatigue or the passing of time, for her thoughts were devotedly oriented in prayers to the Almighty for a year of utmost blessings for the family and especially for Fannie.

With eventide so wistfully setting west, the sun rays blended their shimmering hues against the colorful facade of the stained-glass windows, with Nahama praying her supplications so subtly and devotionally.

When the day-long services were concluded with the blasting sounds of the mystical shofar (ram's horn), Nahama was the last one leaving the Synagogue, holding on to the sanctification of the holy day which she felt would prove most rewarding.

A gorgeous autumn soon drifted into a monotonous, cold, snowy winter, but at the approach of spring the child's prospective arrival began to emerge from a dreamful vision to joyful reality.

It became sheer fun to speculate, will it be a boy or a girl, what color baby outfits to prepare, pink or blue.

THE OMINOUS NIGHT OF BIRTH

A blustery March gave way to a sunny, warm, most pleasant April day on which Fannie began experiencing sporadic labor pains.

A long-time practicing doctor was taking care of Fannie during the pregnancy months and he assured her it would be just as safe and convenient to deliver the baby at home as in any of the regional hospitals, and we followed his advice.

One evening late in April we notified the doctor that the baby's birth seemed imminent and he arrived shortly after.

Fannie was secluded with the doctor in the designated delivery room, and her painful sobbing and moaning were heartbreaking sounds for the family to endure.

But the real moments of anguish came when the doctor worriedly informed us that the baby was positioned to be delivered feet first with possible complications.

At one time the doctor seriously considered summoning professional help, but he felt that his decades of practical experience and known skill would prove sufficient for a safe and successful delivery without any complications.

Unfortunately it proved a grievous misjudgment as he increasingly realized that the unexpected ordeal was gradually taxing his ability and strength.

Fannie's parents, her two brothers and myself were tormentedly pacing the lighted hallways and rooms, praying, crying, with her mother wringing her hands in utmost distress.

I constantly circled around the delivery room, my thoughts numbed in a sheer standstill at the realization of the traumatic events now transpiring.

It was about eleven o'clock in this horrible night when an exhausted doctor called on Fannie's older brother David to assist him.

Stoical and athletically built, he was nevertheless appalled at being confronted by such a terrifying situation.

He became even more increasingly confused by the doctor's strange instructions and was about to rush out and call unheeding neighbors to help when blissfully the doctor managed to deliver the nearly eight-pound baby girl.

With the torment of the child's head being so many hours in a binding stranglehold and suffocating position, the infant's breathing organs were severely damaged.

It was about an hour later when she expired, her pinkish face yet rosy and her head of curly hair yet moist with the dew of a minute-spanned life.

With Fannie's loss of so much blood, her pain and tremendous exhaustion, the doctor lost no time in administering a most potent injection to relieve her anguish and induce sleep.

The doctor advised the family to retire for some rest as Fannie could not in any way be disturbed, and he washed, changed clothes and sat down to keep vigil for a while.

I sat down at the edge of the bed, held her uncovered hand which was restlessly moving and searching as if to feel and touch the gorgeous baby, so tender, so flowery smooth and soft.

So godly perfect from toes to head, but now resting like a fascinating doll, only to fade away soon into earthly demise with dust returning to dust.

With Fannie's face pale and drawn, she whispered weakly on occasion, her words broken and inaudible, then sank back in the trance of captivating, drug-induced sleep.

About two o'clock the doctor left, stating that he would return sometime in the morning.

An eerie oppressive silence had now overtaken this home where but a day before there was a scene of happiness and joyful expectations.

On the same rocker where Fannie dreamfully made plans of putting the baby to sleep, I mournfully watched in the dead of the night, a reflecting glow of the adorable infant waiting for the morning hours to accompany it to the burial ground.

Early morning as the first golden rays of a rising sun began fondly caressing the room's reflective window panes, my mother-in-law, with eyes dry of shedded tears, dejectedly entered the room with Fannie yet in a drugged sleep.

She went over to the crib and her intensive gaze at that child's sacred profile rimmed so fantastically by a growth of jet black wavy hair spoke so soulfully Nahama's wondering thoughts more than any mortal words could say.

Shortly after, her father Nathan sauntered in. He was tall and muscled but his sagging shoulders now reflected so vividly his sinking spirits.

Nearing the child he daintily covered it with a snow-white carriage blanket, which he bought but recently from the samples of a traveling salesman.

He gazed intently for quite a while at the cherished infant and, as he left, turned his head several times for a last goodbye look.

The two brothers, David and Louis, came a few minutes later, biting their lips, standing in a mood of helpless resignation to a destiny found to be gruesome in default.

Months before this tragic day it was decided that if it was a girl she was to be named Frieda (which means joy).

When everyone left I sat down at the edge of the bed again and held tenderly Fannie's dainty hand which after the agonizing ordeal seemed so much more refined and thinner.

I adjusted her wedding ring which was moving loosely on her finger, and I consolingly said, "Thanks to the almighty, he has saved your life. I and you have been blessed by the creator with an abundance of willpower and courage. We are young. Time is a great healer and who knows if we will not in time to come be compensated by providence with a multitude of blessings to atone for this suffering."

"Zelikul," she said. (Zelikul was her nickname for me at times.) "You are a man and can't penetrate the mysteries and feelings of motherhood. Just now I am beyond words of consolation. One thing I diligently learned as a Sunday School teacher and that is you can't question G'd's motives and reasons. But I also learned to have hope and faith, and if we do right by the Almighty, I am certain we will graciously be reciprocated in kind."

It was about ten in the morning when the Chevra Kadisho (those in charge of religious burial) tenderly placed the infant in that white carriage blanket with most of the family accompanying this bizarre funeral entourage to the Tifereth Israel cemetery in Mount Carmel.

For two days the doctor checked Fannie's recuperating condition and on the morning of the third day he stated that Fannie was continually running a high fever for which he could not account.

Instinctively I felt that it was time to consult another doctor with more advanced medical knowledge.

As it happened, a young Jewish Doctor Smigelsky, who was recently discharged from Army duty, had established an office in Mount Carmel.

Not to offend the present doctor, I arranged for them to meet in consultation and it was determined then that Fannie had been stricken by the almost fatal infection of peritonitis.

Grievously he informed the family of the terrible condition confronting us. "There is no cure or antidote to counteract this virulent destructive virus, but if you rush her at once to the Shamokin Hospital, there is a thousand-to-one chance that she may prove one of those fortunates whom nature favors to help."

Dusk was slowly setting in, and in the parting daylight the budding petals on the tree-lined street started to unfold in the scenting warmth of this gorgeous April day.

Fannie gazed meditatingly at that panoramic Divine wonder, her inflamed face and reddened eyes so expressive and illusionary.

The ambulance drew close to the home entrance with Fannie being carried carefully in, while I entered to sit by her side.

Neighbors, some in tears, others with a worried look, had their eyes riveted at this youthful Fannie who only a year after marriage now battled for her very life.

The ten-mile ride to the Shamokin State Hospital was mostly on a bumpy road, and every time the ambulance passed a rotted spot, Fannie moaned from pain it caused her.

Evening was well set in when the head nurse, Mrs. Wardrope, assisted by Mrs. Chlachman, took charge of Fannie and wheeled her in a first-floor corner room where her fate was to be decided in the weeks to come.

Instantly, without wasting any valuable time, they began to

prepare her for the doctor's examination while I paced the surrounding darkened corridors hoping that this would not prove a one-way journey.

It wasn't very long until I saw Doctor George Reese, chief surgeon and director of the hospital, coming down from his second-floor elaborate apartment, heading to examine Fannie.

Tall, above the six-foot mark, rose-colored blond with a profile adorned by a head of luxurious silvery hair, he was a magnificent sight to gaze upon. But what dominated his remarkable personality was his sky-blue smiling Irish eyes that even in tragic moments would propel a spirit of hope that all is not yet lost.

I met him as he descended the stairs and as I greeted him with a handshake, he placed his other hand on my shoulder, telling me that Doctor Smigelski had informed him of the precarious situation and he would see what could be done.

There were many entrances to the hospital but the one facing south led to a tremendous hall decorated with many artful paintings and sculptured statues.

Above huge fireplaces the ornamented heads of deer, buffalo and other stately animals were prominently displayed.

After spending some time with Fannie, Doctor Reese informed me of his great concern about her deteriorating condition. "She will need Divine merciful graciousness and our utmost prayers to recover. This night is most critical. I want you to remain in the hospital and will make the front room available to you. I will arrange so that you will not be disturbed."

The Shamokin State Hospital is erected on a multi-acre woodland ground facing the slanting foothills of the towering North Mountain. Not permitted to visit Fannie until tomorrow, I whiled away the idle time reading and visiting the men's and women's ward patients, many of whom were my customers.

Quite a few times I went out to stroll the winding pathways around the hospital. In these eventful moments of my life the starlit sky and soothing silence seemed so much in tune with the rhythmical, universal splendor.

When I returned I would often pace longingly in the spacious corridors where at times a hurrying nurse would pass me while at a faraway corner the night nurse was absorbed in checking records at a dimly lighted desk.

Once a piercing cry echoed from the women's ward. "Oh Lord, help me I am dying!" While subdued moans from the men's ward permeated the deserted hallways. Instinctively I would go time and again near Fannie's room, though I was not to enter it. The sign of "No visitors allowed, even close relatives" so clearly told the dramatic story of a life-and-death struggle now taking place, the outcome of which it was only for providence to decide.

DRIFTING INTO A DREAM

It was nearing midnight when I went to retire for those eventful night hours. In that luxurious salon the sight of the treasured paintings and alluring animal mountings were so tantalizing. One could hardly imagine that but a short distance away so many mortal humans were fighting to preserve their lives or wondering what destiny had in fate for them, and so I gradually drifted into deep slumber and entered into a dominion of fantastic, dreamy wonderlands that left its magic spell so absorbingly in my thoughts.

Keenly I began to sense a remarkable sensation that I was being gradually released from the earth, freed from its whirling orbit. With a terrifying speed that obliterated the very meaning of swiftness I began passing the planets, the stars of the Milky Way galaxy and the untold constellations in the universal infinity.

Passing me in this celestial splendor were countless humans, also heavenly angels and creatures, remarkably of various shapes, forms and designs, each one seemingly in a hurry with a mission to perform.

Somehow I began to wonder how I survived the numbing cold

and the seering thermal heat as I cruised by their various climatic zones.

Somewhere near a cluster of luminous stars a heavenly angel caught up, instructing me to follow him as we were nearing a planet which would be my final destination.

From sheer absolute weightlessness I began to feel a gravitational pull into the planet's whirling orbit, and soon cascaded into the midst of indescribable beauty.

Surrounding my landing vista were resplendent orchards and gardens with luxurious entertaining facilities. Situated in the center loomed a heavenly palace of ultimate splendor whose towering entrance was luminously inscribed in many languages, "This is the Palace of Justice." Thousands of angels came and went and strangely many were seemingly so different in shape, form, color of their wings or other heavenly ornaments.

One docile angel directed me to follow him and led me to an imposing room in the palace where I was informed that I was here to witness a heavenly trial. In this glowing room of sparkling alabaster and magnificent construction a marble table occupied its exact center with artful chairs, each with an original design, placed all around, with a special artistically ornamented chair at the head of the table.

By the sides of the pearl-white walls, chairs of various patterns were precisely arranged.

Soon many persons began to arrive and, though all had the human outline, they nevertheless were individually different with queer appearances and devious expressions.

We were directed to sit down on the chairs by the wall and I tried to start a conversation with the one nearest to me, but he shook his head and gestured with his long, lanky hands that he couldn't understand me.

About then I had little time left to contemplate what was going on as angels in fantastic garb arrived to sit down around the table, while one in special judge-like raiment occupied the head chair.

A court crier entered and announced that the sessions were in order with everyone rising. The prosecutor's staff seated on the right side of the table was headed by an impressive angel who said, "Your Honor, the first case on the docket is that of Mrs. Fannie Moskowitz from the planet Earth, circling the sun, member of the Milky Way galaxy."

Slowly he began to state that, at the age of four, Fannie was stricken with scarlet fever and was destined to die with her soul assigned to an infant yet to be born on a planet of another constellation. By heavenly grace Fannie was granted a reprieve of sixteen years. Now her present illness was to be her terminal end. I now learned that the angel Gabriel was in the process of asking for another reprieve and that "Your Honor is indeed totally unfair to the unborn child who is waiting to be gifted with Fannie's soul."

The angel attorney for the defense then presented his arguments. "Honorable Judge," he stated, "Fannie's untold humanitarian goodness is indeed priceless. With the prevailing spread of injustice on the planet Earth, such humanitarian persons are indispensable to the earthly communities. Your Honor," he continued, "if that person yet to be born is worthy of Fannie's treasured soul, she would make that great sacrifice and wait until the normally allotted years for a human on earth are ended, and then how much more worthy she will be to inherit Fannie's soul."

The angels argued pro and con until it was getting late and time for an urgent case to begin, so the Judge solemnly postponed the verdict until the next session.

Hypnotized by this fascinating scene, I sat spellbound when the next case came to order. The prosecutor announced the strange name of a middle-aged person, ailing from the constellation "Andromeda." On one of the star's planets, he stated, the inhabitants are so wicked and sinful that there were only nine righteous persons left, and like Sodom and Gomorrah life on its surface was to be destroyed. Then, the prosecutor continued, a venturesome spaceship from another galaxy happened to land on that planet and this person escaped to become a stowaway and managed to disguise his identity to remain there. Being a virtuous person he made a tenth righteous man, preventing thus the destruction of that demonical planet. Day after day the worst atrocities were committed, people killing and murdering each other, and providence could do little to help while this man made up a quorum of righteous people. "I demand Your Honor, that he either leave this planet or pay with his life for his defiance."

The defense angel then rose to state, "Your Honor, like in the Biblical story of Jonah and the Whale, the Lord did everything to save the inhabitants of that great city of Nineveh with its six hundred thousand population. Your Honor," continued the defense angel, "it is self-evident that God motivated this person from another constellation to board an exploring spaceship and join this planet so as to save it from utter destruction. Jonah's mission resulted in that the people of Nineveh repented and became worthy of grace. I am certain that this person is the Lord's emissary who will grant time for the people of that planet to ask for atonement and duly turn to godly ways."

I was anxiously waiting to hear the Judge's verdict when sounds of a speeding ambulance entered the winding hospital roadway leading to the emergency entrance.

It was just a little past five o'clock when it woke me up, but the sudden exciting activity at the hospital and the phenomenal, fantastic dream relating to Fannie's life set my heart and mind in trepidation.

Was the postponement of the heavenly Judge's decision a favorable sign or rather an ominous omen? It instinctively directed me to Fannie's room. I pensively looked at the closed door and wondered if the angel Gabriel was in there preventing "Azrael," the angel of death, from performing his grim mission.

It was now seven o'clock and Doctor Reese, dressed in his operating gown, white buckskin oxfords and tight head cover, was preparing for his morning operations, but he first went to check Fannie's condition and left urgent instructions to the nurses about what to do in those critical hours facing Fannie.

I saw Doctor Reese when he concluded operating about noontime. Mine explosions which brought racing ambulances with the victims added to his burdens with emergency operations, and I wondered if many realized what a saintly accomplishment this noble doctor was performing for mankind.

THE OPERATION

Three weeks later an emergency operation had to be performed on Fannie in order to save her life. It proved to be a three-hour ordeal and with her worn-out body so perilously weakened, unforeseen complications soon developed.

Nurses around the clock, headed by a dedicated Mrs. Shlabinger, were constantly on their tiptoes to take care of minute details that may have meant the difference between life or death.

To relieve somewhat her lack of liquids, moist cloths were applied to her parched lips that quivered appreciatively at their touch.

I was only permitted to see her but a few times a day, and at that only briefly so as not to excite her or sap the little strength that yet remained in her wrecked, tormented body.

Once, during such a momentous visit when she seemed in fever heat delirium, she faintly murmured in Yiddish as I held tenderly her emaciated hand. "God in Himmel (God in heaven) men shtict mir, men drict mir (I am punched and banged) wos willen zei fun myne yunge yoren (what do they want from my young life'').

The nurse then motioned to me that it was time to leave. I indeed left with a lump in my throat and a searing soul in a situation where I could do nothing but get the most qualified medical help and make prayerful supplications to a gracious almighty.

On the morning of the fourth day after the operation, I came early and learned that Doctor Reese had remained in Fannie's room quite longer than usual.

Nervously I now paced the corridors where brisk hospital activities were taking place. It was almost nine o'clock when I saw Doctor Reese leaving her room, followed by the head nurse, Mrs. Wardrope.

I never before had seen Doctor Reese with such a luminous beaming face, his sky-blue Irish eyes sparkling with a heavenly glow.

I met him half way and as I greeted him he embraced my handshake in his soft palms and said, "I think the miraculous turning point in Fannie's recovery may be actually in the making."

Dazzling me with a penetrating, laser-like gaze he stated, "I could not believe myself when I entered her room this morning to examine her condition. She hailed me with a beaming smile that was priceless to me. If anyone who went through the agonizing torment almost beyond a human capacity to endure could yet summon the will power and courage to smile, she is surely inscribed in the heavenly records for treasured life."

"Can I go in and see her now, doctor?" I inquired impatiently.

"No, not until later, for there is much to be done until she is actually out of danger."

But actually this was indeed a gross understatement of a noble, accomplished doctor who had his heart and soul set to save Fannie's life, and the wish duly became the mother of his thought.

For the fact is that the memorable hospital's corner room remained Fannie's recuperating home for many months more to come.

During those trying weeks there were fluctuations in her condition, with most of the time nurses in watchful vigilance against a sudden upset.

The great day finally came in early August when Doctors Reese and Buczko, many devoted nurses and hospital patients came to bid Fannie a cordial farewell. There were beaming smiles everywhere expressing the thought that seemingly the creator's monumental miracles were not a myth or dreamful illusion. But Doctor Reese expressed it best stating that Fannie's incomparable courage and willpower was what moved the Divine powers to say bravo to one deserving priceless life and health.

MOVING TO SHAMOKIN

For nearly five months I had spent a great deal of time with Fannie in the hospital, thus neglecting considerably my ongoing business.

Driving daily from Shamokin and Mount Carmel had also proved an extra burden to endure, so now we thought it was time to move to Shamokin, and we soon rented a second-floor apartment in the Turner building on Market Street.

For Fannie, to assume the responsibility of housekeeping was also recommended by her doctors.

Being kept busy they said, would not leave her much time to dwell on the previous distressful memories.

For the first time Fannie wasn't pampered as when her parents were always at hand to help with meals and other housework services.

In our newly furnished apartment we felt now like two youngsters experimenting with a beautiful new toy.

But it seems providence has a way to complicate matters to those in the least need of it and it chose again Fannie as its target.

We were in our new home but ten days when Fannie responded to a knock on the door, opening it readily as she was always so used to doing in Mount Carmel.

Facing her was a young man, clean shaven, of medium height and shifty eyes, who hastened to ask her if she knew where the people who resided there before had moved.

Instantly sensing something wrong in his wandering gaze, she quickly told him that she could not be of any help but that Mr. Turner, who lived downstairs, would surely know.

Her fears soon were justified when he advanced further in the room blocking somehow Fannie's opportunity to get out.

Changing the subject of looking for someone he boldly said, "You certainly are an extremely attractive woman."

Realizing now the mortal danger facing her, she bravely circled the dining room table to be closer to the door, but he quickly outmaneuvered her.

Stalling for time Fannie said, "You came to inquire about someone, I don't know them, now why don't you leave and avoid trouble for me and you?"

"Why don't you be nice to me," he calmly said. "Do I look like a monster?"

"Just because you consider yourself a gentleman you should leave and prevent misfortune for me and you."

Ignoring her advice, he asked her, "Where is the key to the door?"

"Mr. Turner is making a new one for me so, you see, there is none."

"I aim to do you no harm but you better come with me to the bedroom or you may get hurt."

Fannie tried again to run around the table but, seemingly enraged now, he warned her not to try it again.

He was on the verge of cornering her when a hard knock on the door stopped him in his tracks.

"Come in," shouted Fannie, loud and sure.

In came Reverend Janowsky, the Jewish community teacher and ritual chicken slaughterer.

Standing six feet high and then some, black-bearded with piercing black eyes, he rivaled the legends of sea priates on the loose, and at the very sight of him the man left without wasting time on a parting goodbye.

That Reverend Janowsky not only had the looks of a giant but also the temper of a hot-headed Oriental.

He was the father of eleven children and had a docile wife who believed in the virtue of motherhood.

Once, when on several occasions he did not receive his monthly pay on time, he led his entire family, including his wife, to the City Hall to shame the Jewish community's tardiness in paying wages.

When he learned now what had transpired, he flashed out of his coat pocket the ritual knife and placed it at his throat, and he vowed that was what he would have done to that wretched bum.

"I would have killed him and the law would be on my side. He may have had a deadly weapon with him," he exclaimed.

Fannie had a chicken in the cellar to slaughter so he went down, finished the job, waited for the chicken to stop bleeding, then wrapped it in newspaper and brought it up to the apartment.

About that time a nearby hardware store sent up a worker to install a sliding latch and that apartment door never again opened until the person was identified through the remaining narrow open space.

When I came home and she told me the harrowing story, I was wondering what more terrifying dark corners we had to pass in order to test our faith and love for the Almighty.

Later that night I told her a Talmudic tale that on account of a quarrel about a hen and rooster, the city of Bethar with a four hundred thousand population was destroyed.

"And today in contrast, on account of slaughtering a chicken, your very life may have been saved."

IV

Venturing in Real Estate

Success as a rule motivates greater efforts and it seemed to hold true with me, so when the opportunity presented itself to purchase a liquidating household goods store at a bargain price, I gave it serious consideration.

I consulted with the bank's president, Mr. Greaber, and explained to him that the store had a line of merchandise handled by the Washington Mills that I had managed and thus I could make the store a going proposition.

He thought that it was a sensible move and suggested that I buy the building, which the bank was to sell for delinquent mortgage payments by the present owner.

Fannie and her parents thought it was a fair proposition and within weeks the deal was made, with another store and building to boot.

I moved into the building's apartment and rented out a small store next to the one I was to open. On one occasion I was referred to as landlord and somehow it sounded quite embarrassing to me when I recalled that only five years before I was awkwardly jobless.

Unlike my profitable footwear business, this venture couldn't get off the ground floor.

Its shortcomings dawned on me with the first opening day sale.

I realized then that I had a variety of merchandise, but not a desirable selection of sizes, colors and so on.

The location too was a bit away from the business section and the manager fell short of expectations.

Knowing that recognizing a losing proposition is the most sensible thing to do, I sold the store and building within a year, almost recouping my original investment.

We could have remained in the apartment but it was entirely too large for us and the rooms' arrangements were very awkward and quite impractical.

We began looking now for a home and some months later bought a corner house on the tranquil tree-lined Dewart Street, where the sun's circling sunshine made its glorious presence felt all day long.

Though this too was a large house, having two floors and an attic, we did not hesitate to buy it, for a very good and inspiring reason.

Since the day Fannie returned home from that prolonged confinement at the hospital, we had been wondering what the prospects were of raising a family.

We consulted many doctors who, generally, warned us that childbirth could prove fatal.

Then, about two years later, we went to consult a Philadelphia gynecology specialist to get his expert opinion, which we vowed to follow.

At his imposing Walnut Street office he gave Fannie an extensive hour-long examination, occasionally checking the Shamokin hospitals chart.

At the conclusion he went to his desk to update the records and form his decision.

Those passing moments of stifling silence seemed like an eternity to us as we wondered what the verdict would be, that of sheer hopelessness or, in contrast, dreamlike joy.

The professor, who closely resembled John Chancellor of television fame, came over, sat down next to Fannie and said, "My dear lady, there is no reason whatsoever to avoid childbirth.

"In fact, if any wastage has remained in your body after the operation, it will be dislodged with a blessed childbirth."

We thanked him profusely as we left this monumental place that held so much promise for us in the future.

So we now bought this loveable home with an unreserved faith that, within its confines, the priceless gift of God would hopefully come our way. And blissfully it came to pass that our daughter, Meta, and son, Myron, were born while we were residing there.

We bought this lovely Dewart Street home with an abiding faith that the Almighty would compensate us for the grievous loss of Frieda, and how wonderful it felt to see this Divine blessing prove so splendidly true indeed.

DARKENING SKIES

Looking back now on the chronicles of my life, it is no wonder that this wonderful destiny soon turned darkened by swiftly gathering clouds.

For, all through my unchartered life's journey, there was an unfailing pattern that, after a providential blessing, there surely followed a reversal, sometimes severe and at other times in a milder form.

So now, when the jubilant news of hopefully raising a family filled our hearts with indescribable rejoicing, there had to be a joy-killer and indeed it was not long in coming.

It began when a group of five businessmen formed a real estate company and bought the triangle corner of the Greamar Hotel where my store was located. They didn't waste any time and tripled my store rent.

I had good reason to believe that they aimed eventually to evict me and rent the store to a relative of one of them to open a shoe-store and take over my established trade.

Just then there was a building for sale on Independence Street, right across from the Reading Railroad Station.

It had two large stores and some apartments, with one store lease having only a year to go, after which I could take it over.

I went to consult with Mr. Greaber, who was frank in telling me that the bank would be reluctant to finance a deal where a nearly forty-thousand dollar mortgage would be required.

At that time I became acquainted with Mr. Unger, President of the very progressive Market Street National Bank.

I went one day and explained to him my complicated situation and asked him if he could be of any help to me.

"I will let you know after the board of directors' meeting on Tuesday," he said.

I felt my chances of getting it were quite good, for the directors usually followed his recommendations.

Indeed this is exactly what happened, with Mr. Unger advising me that they would finance me with a bank mortgage if I invested ten thousand dollars of my own.

A few weeks later the transaction was duly consummated and the valuable property was deeded to me and Fannie.

I felt it was a daring challenge and was indeed proud of the accomplishment.

A period of but several months passed and then the building was burned down.

It was then that it was discovered that the bank had failed to insure the mortgage at its full value.

The sensible thing for me to have done was to let the bank have the building, taking my ten-thousand-dollar investment loss in stride and making the best of a difficult situation.

But property values in Shamokin had steadily heightened, and when Mr. Unger assured me that the bank would re-finance the structure's rebuilding, I decided to go along with that and take my chances.

It turned out to be a very bad decision, for what seems at times right theoretically, proves altogether wrong in practical life.

For, to my misfortune, a carpenters' strike delayed the rebuilding for a greater part of the year.

During that wasted time the mortgage interest had to be paid, and other expenses piled up, draining my business assets to a perilous point.

I felt I had one foot in an economic swamp, and how to prevent my other foot from getting entrapped was indeed a problem with seemingly no answers at that present time.

I recalled my boastful statement many years before that I seem to have acquired the King Midas Touch, and Fannie had cautioned me not to brag. How right she truly was, I thought.

For the first time I had no line of business credit at the bank, since they were devoting all their financing to the structure's rebuilding.

I could not pay my bills on time anymore and had to resort to borrowing on my life insurance policies, paying both premiums and costly interest.

It was at that time that my brother in New York, finding himself out of work, came to visit me and, as my steady clerk was leaving to enter a school of pharmacy, it dawned on us that it would be of mutual benefit to work together in the store.

In New York he had been employed as a pocketbook maker, and as I expected soon to move into my new store on Independence Street, it would prove of mutual benefit to both of us.

ASSURANCE OF A FRIEND

But it was that month of October when I was about to move into my new store that proved to be the beginning of what turned out to be decades of untold struggle descending ever more into an abyss from which it seemed only gracious divine miracles could save me.

In order to make a good showing in the new store, I had to buy new window display fixtures, shoe benches and other necessities which proved to be more expensive than I had originally anticipated. As a result I left two months' rent unpaid on the corner store I was in.

One day I met the president of the five partners who owned the property and told him that on November First I would be moving to my new location, and as I expected a check from a good friend of mine in New York to arrive shortly, I would be sure to take care of the two months' rent without delay. (The friend who would mail me a check was the Mr. Schwartz who introduced me to Fannie.)

"Don't you worry about it," he said, "you are not running out of town and, after all, aren't we long time friends?"

I heartily shook hands with him, and each of us left to do our intended tasks.

A week later, on a rainy September day when I left home on my way to the store, I saw Sheriff Shively coming up the street. He waved to me as if to wait. The sidewalk was covered thick with fallen leaves, causing him to slip several times, but he managed to hold his balance.

Sheriff Shively was a lifelong miner and during a colliery explosion had lost an arm. Later he became interested in politics and finally was elected to the lucrative position of County Sheriff.

When he met me he said sadly, "Ely, I am sorry to serve you these foreclosure papers, but it is my duty to follow the law."

"Foreclosure!" I exclaimed. "Foreclosure on what?" I wanted to know.

He managed with his one hand to get out the store lease that gave the owners the right to padlock the store without any previous warning.

"Here are the payments due, two months' rent with added interest and seventy-eight dollars sheriff expenses. If you can pay it in full you are in the clear."

Fannie observed us talking, but naturally had no idea what it was all about.

I asked him to go with me to the store. There I called Mr. Unger and informed him of the developing situation.

"I cannot give you a bank loan as your credit is already way overextended, but I will give you a personal check to cover the amount necessary to avoid padlocking the store."

I then left with Sheriff Shively for Mr. Unger's office, where the distressful episode was taken care of thanks to Mr. Unger's friendship and generosity.

I told Mr. Unger about the talk I had with the head man of the building partners and the shock I got when the promise was so greivously broken.

"You obviously have had no time to read United States history," he said.

"People have been dispossessed on the mere pretense of a legal error or a misspelled word in a contract.

"There is no limit as to what people will do to gain power and wealth. You should be glad that you are learning your lesson while you are young, just as long as you remember it."

IN THE NEW STORE

In early November 1925 I had the new store's opening sale with much success.

The better business location and greater inventory made it possible to accommodate a larger clientele, and during the following months sales almost doubled.

But the building, with its large mortgage and unforeseen other expenses, drained the added store's profits, thus not improving my financial position.

During the following three years Fannie gave birth to another daughter and a son, and she lost no time outlining the profession they were suited for.

Every Halloween we would give a party for the B'nai Israel congregation's children at the synagogue's social hall, as the four children we had by then had been born in the Autumn.

The costumes Fannie designed for the girls were that of nurses, a surgeon's gown for one son and that of a judge for the other.

In 1932 another daughter was born, and when she began dressing up for the Halloween parties, she too was dressed as a nurse.

In the decades that followed the younger son graduated as a doctor, two daughters graduated as nurses, and my oldest daughter graduated as a pharmacist and my oldest son as an attorney.

When I asked her how she guessed what destiny meant them to be, she merely said it was a sense of intuition.

While I was busy manipulating my business and financial problems, Fannie was occupied planning the children's future.

Since her early youth, she had been addicted to the piano and loved music, so the children had to master it as well.

They all learned to play the piano. In addition, Meta, the oldest, played the accordion, Myron the clarinet, Marquita the cello, Roland the oboe and Cleo, the youngest, the accordion and violin.

Business conditions did not warrant this added expense for musical instruments and teaching, so for a while it was kept a secret from me.

The first time I learned of this extravagance was when the synagogue ran a social affair with home talent entertainment.

I was sitting comfortably enjoying the various acts when the master of ceremonies said, "Now we will have Meta Moskowitz play some numbers on the accordion."

For a while I thought I was dreaming. I looked around to see if I was really where I was supposed to be in the synagogue social, but had very little time to think about anything as I saw Meta with a smiling face, her luxurious long hair reflecting exciting youth with a mission to perform, walking up on the stage steps to present her part of the entertainment program.

I was ashamed to make any comments about being ignorant

about my daughter playing. All I was interested in now was that she didn't make a fool out of herself.

"The first number Meta will play," announced the master of ceremonies, will be 'Let me call you sweetheart I'm in love with you.' "

I recalled now that this was the tune Fannie had played when I first came to Mount Carmel to meet her.

With the first tuneful notes I knew I had nothing to worry about, and when she had played three numbers she was hailed with loud exclamations of bravos, being recalled by a tremendous applause for an encore.

I went over to congratulate her as though I had known her musical abilities for years.

"You would have come to know it sometime and this was the most exciting way to surprise you," Fannie said gleefully.

In time the children formed their own orchestra and I became accustomed to the blaring sounds, but at times it made me take an extra walk to escape the upheaval.

FANNIE BEGINS WORKING IN THE STORE

It was during the end of the eventful 1930s that Fannie decided to help in the store to save on extra clerks, usually hired during Saturdays, paydays and pre-holidays.

It was also during those years that my in-laws had to liquidate their business and Fannie's new preoccupation gave her less time to think about the unpleasantness of life.

We were fortunate, though, that our children, even in their early youth, matured to realize our difficult economic conditions and appreciated it more so when we went out of our way to try to make them content and happy.

It was during the end of that decade that I also determined that my fifty-thousand-dollar indebtedness on the building would eventually mire me in an economic swamp.

So I informed the bank to take over the property since they held the mortgage.

It was later on sold to someone who needed my storeroom. I was then forced to move to a less desirable location, which reduced my business considerably.

It was during those trying times that I ventured to open another outlet on Market Street, but I soon discovered that having two stores in one small community merely meant dividing my clientele with yet added expenses, so I lost no time liquidating it, fortunately without loss.

During that time my brother married, increasing considerably his living expenditures, so when the opportunity presented itself to open another store in Mount Carmel, I did not hesitate to take that chance.

I then took charge of the Mount Carmel store, with Fannie and my brother taking care of the one in Shamokin.

Unfortunately, the years of the great 1930s depression descended with all their rueful implications.

Credits tightened, margins of profit reduced, and business at best was a constant struggle against ever bolder competition.

As I look back at those eventful years I can't stop wondering how Fannie and I found the willpower and time to devote ourselves to religious, charitable and social activities.

THE TURBULENT WORLD CONDITION

As for me personally, the turbulent world conditions dogged me persistently to the point of torment.

Those were the years when Stalin and Hitler invented the demonic scourge of the "Big Lie."

It ran roughshod in a confused world beset by massive unemployment, social unrest, stark poverty and most of all by political instability.

In such a venomous atmosphere the Big Lie rooted itself deeply in the fertile ground of human vexation and distress.

The bigger the lie, the more readily it seemed to have been accepted by gullible people who reasoned that no sensible person would dare proclaim such ridiculous impossibilities unless there was some truth in them.

How much people are prepared to abdicate their godgiven sense of reasoning in face of accomplished facts, I had occasion to remember in later years to come after the following episode.

I was on my way one time from Mount Carmel to Shamokin on a trolley car during a blackout night. At a Brady stop, a stout lady got on and sat down near the trolley's operator. After a short conversation about the war, she finally said, "The United States had no business entering the conflict. Hitler must be surely right in what he is planning and doing or he wouldn't be so successful."

"You said it, I am with you all the way," replied the trolley operator. "There seems to be no end to his conquests," he added.

That defeatist, submissive conversation lingered long in my thoughts until the final defeat of Hitler erased it from my mind.

During those momentous years while I was busy at times making loans to cover incoming checks in the bank, I was equally occupied writing letters to metropolitan newspapers refuting the poisonous propaganda of the hideous Hitler Era.

I had more than a hundred letters published in the *Philadelphia Record* with timely comments on world affairs.

I dealt extensively with the wholesale shoe firm Vanity Shoe Company. One of the partners in the firm was Mr. Jerry Kimmelman.

He told me that one time he had lunch in a downtown Philadelphia restaurant and he overheard Mr. Stern, owner and publisher of the *Philadelphia Record,* saying to the paper's editor, "I have a notion to get in contact with Mr. Moskowitz suggesting that he contribute a weekly column in the paper."

About a month later it ceased publication. I often wondered if Mr. Stern's wish would have materialized had the paper continued its publication.

Fannie, being more pragmatic than I was, was busy helping humanity in our mining region where assisting the needy was a daily chore.

Also occupying a great deal of her time was sending out get-well cards to hospital patients.

For during her five-month confinement in the hospital she noted the nagging loneliness of those who seldom received cheerful get-well wishes.

She then faithfully resolved that if a gracious almighty granted her life, she would make it certain that those unfortunate persons would not be forgotten.

That benevolent mission she trustfully fulfilled for fifty-five years of her eventful life until she returned to her maker in 1975.

Helping miners' families in time of need was a self-assumed mission she so devotedly performed.

One episode that I still remember well occurred a few days before Christmas.

A developing snowstorm prompted me to leave Mount Carmel earlier than usual, and when I arrived in the Shamokin store, Fannie was waiting on a miner whose sickly look presaged a black lung condition.

He had with him six children, but asked Fannie to fit up only the two older girls.

"How about the others?" inquired Fannie, noting the wornout shoes on their feet.

"You see, Fannie (just call me Fannie she always asked her customers), I am working at the Scott Colliery in Kulpmont, we are still on strike and I have had no pay for more than a month. I must buy for the older girls and will then have some money left to purchase food for the holiday."

Without wasting any time, Fannie told him that no child would ever leave that store without getting new shoes for Christmas.

"I am not even going to mark it in the book, you will pay me when you are able to."

A glistening tear rolled down his rock-dust shriven face, his effort to thank her stuck in a choking throat.

Remarkably Fannie had very insignificant losses with about ninety percent of the bills being paid up in the course of time.

Under the skilled leadership of the miners' union president, John L. Lewis, the miners' working and earning conditions made considerable progress, but it hardly made a dent in what was really required to advance their general living conditions.

John L. Lewis actually admitted that to me in a letter written on March 17, 1937.

What made me write him and receive that letter in reply was a painful incident in February of that year.

I was busy in my Mount Carmel store rearranging the stock with the clerk, Victoria Dempshock, waiting on a lady customer when in came a boy, age about twelve, wearing one regular shoe and another man-sized.

"What's wrong?" I asked him.

"My mom just had a baby in the hospital and my father is home taking care of the children. A couple of days ago I stepped on a rusted nail and the foot is swelling up. My dad wants to know if you will give me a pair of bedroom slippers until pay day."

I told him to sit down and take off his man's shoe, and when I took one look at his swollen foot, I realized his life was in danger from the deadly possibility of lockjaw.

I gave him a pair of bedroom slippers, then called Doctor Smigelsky to say I was sending a boy up, to take care of him and to send me the bill.

I then wrote to John L. Lewis asking him why the union had no medical insurance plan to prevent such a case where a child's life is in jeopardy due to a miner's poverty.

It was to this letter that he replied, "My Dear Mr. Moskowitz, I am in receipt of your letter of March 11th and I was much interested in your comments on the condition of the Anthracite Coal Miners.

"I am glad to have your point of view on this subject and I realize that there is a great deal of truth in what you say.

"The United Mine Workers of America are doing as they have done in the past everything in their power to improve the wages, hours and working conditions of their members in the Anthracite Coal fields.

"We cannot accomplish the superhuman but we do what we can. Signed, sincerely yours, John L. Lewis."

In the years to come he did make a special effort to advance the miners' economic standing, but unfortunately it was by means of general strikes.

For those were the decades when oil and gas made tremendous inroads as energy fuels, and when coal shortages occurred due to the strikes, the competitive resources took coal's place.

THE CLOSING OF MINES

Soon, mine after mine began to close, their abandoned gangways, tunnels, shafts and caverns quickly flooded with sulphuric waters dooming its reopening possibilities actually beyond recourse.

With these closings started a new era of stripping and bootleg mining.

It was the bootleg mining that tested men's willpower and courage to provide a livelihood for them and their families, no matter what the cost was in human life, labor and toil.

A few individuals or a small group would rent a plot of ground from a coal company, starting an enterprise on their own.

They would begin sinking a slope, at times at a dangerously slanting degree, the depth unknown until the precious coal vein loomed into view.

Having no return ventilation, special care had to be taken to avoid gas explosions.

In rainy seasons timber supports would often give way, demolishing in a few minutes the painstaking toil and labor it had taken years to build.

But it was the lives lost in such catastrophic collapses that mattered most.

It left families in bereavement without a breadwinner and at times without hope.

But the hardy miners, accustomed to persevere in hardships and disaster, would not give up as they constantly challenged fate to start rebuilding again in the depths of the mountain fastnesses that hold the precious deposits of anthracite coal.

Many of those bootleg miners often had to wait months before they could mine and sell a ton of coal and required credit to hold them over that difficult period.

And as I look back to those eventful years, I feel proud that Fannie and I went all out to help them in the time of need.

DEPRESSION YEARS

During those depression years there were many stranded pedestrians passing through Shamokin, and the Jewish congregation had a special fund to help their most urgent needs as much as possible.

It also provided, at times, queer and exciting moments.

One such episode happened when an elderly person just wanted a railroad ticket to get him to New York, which he got.

A few days later Mr. Smith, the ticket agent of the Reading Railroad, told me that a man had bought tickets to New York at Mount Carmel, Shenandoah, Mahonoy City and many other towns, cashing them in later and saying he was going back to Chicago.

It was an isolated incident that never repeated itself, but its ingenuity deserved a salutary thought.

A more serious incident took place one Friday when a middle-aged, tall, gaunt man, wearing an oversized army coat, came to ask for help.

We already had three persons registered in the National Hotel for an overnight lodging, so we gave him money for food and advised him to leave for Mount Carmel and remain there for the Sabbath day.

On Saturday morning I received a call from the State Police Barracks that a tall man wearing an army coat was killed on a railroad track near Excelsior.

The man was circumcised and seemed to be Jewish.

According to the Talmudic law, the town nearest where a person is killed is to take charge of burial rites.

All indications pointed to the fact that the wanderer was the one killed.

He was taken to the Lucas Funeral Parlor where I went to see if I could recognize him.

Since he was somewhat mutilated, no positive identification could be made, but his height, body shape and the army coat were evidently the same as those of the transient person.

We called Rabbi David Silver in Harrisburg for advice, and he said that while all indications were that it would be proper to bury him in the Jewish cemetery, he would wait a while to give his final decision.

No sooner did he hang up the telephone when the State Police called to inform me that a Rasberry Hill woman had identified the man as her missing husband and the mystery was thus solved.

A unique and fanciful episode occurred once on a hot day in July.

Fannie was in the Shamokin store when two Rabbis collecting funds for a Jerusalem Yeshivah came looking for her.

They seemed in every way an extreme contrast. One was tall,

broad-shouldered and black-bearded while the other was short, stout with a reddish beard.

As there is no Kosher restaurant in Shamokin, they wanted to know if she could prepare them a dairy meal.

Our apartment was then above the store so she gladly agreed to accommodate them.

She prepared them some eggs, Russian-style Borscht in jars by Rokeach, and also tea and Kosher cake for dessert.

They then washed up and refreshed themselves in that scorching July day and before they left they thanked her profusely for her generosity and asked her if there was anything special she would wish for in her life.

Unhesitatingly she told them to give her a Brocho (blessing) that her three daughters should marry young.

With eyes half closed they said a prayer in Hebrew and assured her that, since she was such a noble person, they were certain a gracious almighty would grant her the wish.

Remarkably their blessing came true. Two daughters married at eighteen and another missed it by a year with her marital union taking place at nineteen.

But Fannie could never forgive herself for not including our two sons in the Brocho.

Painstakingly she watched the passing years rolling by with no sign in sight of their intention of plighting their troth.

To her joyful relief, both finally found their destined life partners, one at the age of thirty-two and the other at forty.

I surely thought they were to remain old bachelors, she often commented with an expressive sigh of easement.

EXCURSIONS TO NEW YORK

In the midst of the economic trials and tribulations, the children nevertheless missed very few exciting pleasures in an active life.

More often than not it was our spacious eight-room apartment above the store that was the gathering place of their friends.

With containers of potato chips and pretzels abounding they would make themselves comfortable on the floor and sofas, listening to various radio programs—the Lone Ranger, western tales, Amos and Andy, and such thrilling mystic exclamations as "the Shadow Knows." Practicing music lessons left the house in a turmoil and helping each other with school homework made time pass quickly.

The boys would often be caught overhearing the girls whispering secrets and complaints about which of them dominated the bathroom.

On Saturday mornings at least one boy had to attend synagogue services and who was supposed to go a certain Saturday was a problem I often had to solve.

Going to the movies each child tried to get an extra nickel or dime by claiming his or her special performance in the store, on errands or at home deserved it.

In the end Fannie gave them all extra money for peanuts or candy.

When Meta and Marquita entered the teenage years, the boys often complained that boyfriends spoiled them by treating them profusely.

"You boys have other advantages," Fannie reprimanded them. This trait of human jealousy seems not to escape many, I thought.

But one of the most pleasuresome events in those formative family years was the railroad excursions to New York City, which were truly exciting.

Those excursions on the Reading Railroad were made up of about ten passenger coaches, which usually left Shamokin on Saturdays at midnight, arriving at the sprawling Jersey City terminal early Sunday morning.

With five children to settle down, we were always there on time so we were sure of each getting a seat.

With more than five hundred people, mostly of the younger generation out to have a good time, the crowded cars soon became a bedlam of hilarious turmoil.

Many had flasks of whiskey, either in their back pockets or ready in hand, getting a stimulating sip then and there as they wandered from car to car, leaving the doors from one to another open.

The several conductors with their usual previous experience did not even try to make a semblance of order.

After they collected the tickets, they got busy checking records and figures, minding their own business.

As the night progressed, many began marching in groups, singing Polish, Italian, Ukrainian and English songs, having the time of their life.

With the car doors open, the belching columns of the engine's acrid smoke rolled in freely in the crowded coaches, but the worst was yet to come when the train entered the mile-long Mahanoy Mountain tunnel, and when it emerged from that suffocating entrapment, there was a prolonged spell of coughing.

About that time everyone looked like a miner leaving for home after a day's toil in the coal and rock dust.

Fannie, anticipating such a condition, had wet towels prepared to clean up and others to dry the hands and face.

Strangely, the children considered it lots of fun, enjoying the exciting experience until Morpheus lulled them to sleep and very seldom awakening before we reached our final destination at Jersey City in the morning.

We waited until the awakened multitude, now seemingly so docile and orderly, left the cars with the children little by little getting up and heading for the ferry that would take us to New York City across the river.

We had our schedule all made up for the exciting day's activities.

In hot summer days crossing with the ferry was an invigorating event. A soft breeze from the sea was so stimulating indeed.

Reaching New York we took the subway for Forty-Second Street and Broadway, where Hector's Cafeteria was truly a life saver.

It occupied an immense corner. The rest rooms in the basement were meticulously clean, with ample facilities to wash up and refresh.

The selection of food and delicacies seemed of endless varieties, all kinds of cheese cake and superb danish pastry, their known specialty.

After a resplendent breakfast we headed to my parents' home in Brooklyn.

They resided on the second floor in an old tenement building in a three-room flat.

My father would even interrupt his prayers to welcome us and my noble mother got busy embracing, kissing and loving each child as a newfound treasure to behold.

She would reach for the cubbyhole where she kept her meager funds, get some money and hasten to the corner store in the same building, buying fresh rolls and all that went with them.

There was only one time that an unpleasant scene developed. It was Passover, when only Matzo and no bread is eaten.

Of late certain baked cakes had been permitted to be served but my father never agreed with the new procedure.

On one of our visits on Passover week, my younger son, then age five, had a piece of such cake with him and my father said, "If you want to eat it, go outside in the hall."

"No," my son said, "if I can't eat it it's not right eating it anywhere, and if I can eat it outside, why can't I have it here?"

I tried to convince the child to go out with me to the hall and stubbornly he refused, which somehow angered my father.

My mother felt grieved by this unexpected incident and it took the joy out of the visit.

But when we left all was smoothed out with ardent kisses and embracing, breaking a spell of prevailing human emotions.

From our parents' home we usually went to see the sights of

Radio City, the rising skyscrapers and many other things, and then went back again to Hector's for dinner.

It was a self-service cafeteria so we all got trays and each selected what we wanted.

One Sunday they had a special on small capon chickens and everyone decided on that delicacy with some vegetables added.

Cleo, the youngest, then age five, led the march of our seven-member family with capons on our trays, and the crowded cafeteria focused their gaze on us, probably thinking it was an advertising gimmick of some enterprising chicken firm.

When the railroad company finally gave up the excursions as a losing proposition, we really missed them.

ENTERING THE 1940s

Entering the 1940s I encountered monumental years that tremendously changed the course of our lives.

The bank that rented me the store decided to build a branch on the corner where part of my store was.

There was not a place in town to be rented, so I had to be satisfied with the part that remained.

I moved some of the stock to Mount Carmel where I had ample space and would bring back daily to the Shamokin store the most necessary items.

The most trying fact was that on busy days I could not accommodate seating capacity for my customers.

The part that was left to me was in bad shape, the walls were cracking, the ceiling peeling, and it was in a condition actually beyond repair possibilities.

Business kept on steadily declining and it came to the point where my credit constantly deteriorated.

A major part of a shoestore business was miners' gum boots. There were two brands that dominated the market, that of

"Goodrich" and "Ballband." It was indispensable to have them.

Without Goodrich or Ballband it would have been like a grocery store without sugar or bread.

That year of 1940 Mr. Baired, the Ballband salesman, came as usual and took my order but it was never shipped to me.

The following week Mr. Lighthouser from the Goodrich rubber company came as usual and took my order, but here again it was never shipped.

I got in touch with the credit managers by telephone to assure them that their bills would be taken care of on time, but did not get any satisfactory answer.

I could not remain long in business without those products so I got a friend of mine in Philadelphia to order them for me.

Of course it entailed extra expenses that I was glad to pay, for it was indeed a must situation.

MY BROTHER LEAVES FOR HAZLETON

With my brother married now, it remained quite impossible under such difficult business conditions to provide a livelihood for two families, so my brother decided on moving to Hazleton where he joined the scrap metal business his in-laws had conducted for many decades.

Fannie then took full charge of the Shamokin store, determined to make it a paying place.

It was also the years when the United States entered the war, and when Myron graduated from high school he was soon drafted into the army.

Those were times that truly tested men's spirits and souls.

With the despotic dictatorships of Stalin and Hitler, the continents of Europe, Africa and Asia were practically dominated by them.

The political and military situations were deteriorating day by day for those who remained in the democratic fold.

The United States was then the only beacon of light sending a message of hope and encouragement for a humanity beset with fear and anguish.

In those critical times I was ever more moved to write letters to newspapers, magazines and other periodicals stating that the human spirit at the end had always proved victorious and that the scourge of hatred and bigotry was bound to meet its doom if we only persevered and were willing to make the painful, ultimate sacrifices.

But more so than the media, I corresponded with senators, governors, congressmen and many other influential political leaders, to urge unity and prevent quislings and Communists from discouraging our war efforts.

Our land now remained the only beacon of light for humanity to be guided by.

A RAY OF LIGHT AMID DARKNESS

Even in times of untold stress and upheaval the daily life of mankind seems to cope with its constant problems, and in the midst of my ever-present struggle, a brilliant shaft of glorious sunshine came our way when Meta now graduated at the age of nineteen from the Temple University School of Pharmacy.

It was Fannie's lifelong ambition to give her children the adequate education providence had so cruelly denied her. Furthermore, she saw the importance of a profession for a permanent foundation in life's vulnerable uncertainties.

Now she was privileged to witness the first fruits of her efforts. Meta depended on her from day to day for her college subsistence.

On the Reading train, The Cannonball, that left Shamokin for Philadelphia every day at 9:27 in the morning, Fannie would give the conductor at times food packages and sometimes an envelope with a dollar or two, and Meta would wait for it at the Philadelphia terminal when the train arrived there.

For money was scarce, every dollar counted and was badly needed to make good checks in the bank.

Often we waited impatiently to terminate a sale, at times selling the shoes at a loss in order to rush with the money needed for a deposit that had to be made before three o'clock.

It also became necessary at times to send money from Mount Carmel by the trolley car in a shoe box which we waited for in Shamokin so we could rush with it to deposit it in the bank before the checks would be returned.

There was a two dollar-protest charge on such returned checks besides the setback it would give to my already badly shaken credit rating.

No wonder that Meta's graduation in those bleak years was an event to brighten the murky economic skies.

Meta too felt a thrilling sense of accomplishment, for it was a challenge that required her initiative and utmost help.

After school she worked late hours in drugstores to help with her earnings for the ongoing expenses.

Once she went out with a girlfriend shopping for a dress and for almost a week she looked for all kinds of excuses to delay the purchase as it seemed difficult for her to part with the six dollars she had saved to buy it with.

At one time she and a girlfriend were invited to Cleveland for a date with students in a dental school.

Meta already had the proper clothes to wear but no train fare.

Realizing our financial bind, she was reluctant to ask mother for it. She finally took courage and promised that she would soon repay it with her prospective earnings.

In this letter of appreciation I am publishing, you can see the sterling character of an ambitious girl who was destinated to succeed beyond any words.

Phila., Penna.   Sunday afternoon
Dec. 13, 1942

Dear Mother:

    Mother, I don't like to get over sentimental, but I can't keep to myself how much I love you. You're just so wonderful that I have to tell how I feel. You can't understand the feeling I got when I received your letter this week, telling me if I wanted to go to Cleveland you'd manage somehow. I realize how hard it is for you and yet you never complained. I showed Vida your letter. She agreed with me about how wonderful you are. Gosh, how many mothers would have done the same thing. I just have to tell you that I realize I'm the luckiest girl in the whole world. I have everything anyone could possibly ask for and more. I belong to a family that can't be beat. To me, Mother, you're truly one in a million! Daddy does what he can for us if he has it, my brothers and sisters I'm tremendously proud of. We aren't an ordinary family. I am one of a selected few who can go to college. I'll be a pharmacist at 19 which is a distinction—how many girls can boast that. I admit we aren't rich materially, but, Mother, we have riches that extend far beyond, riches that can't be bought. Oh gosh, I'm afraid I'm so full emotionally. I want to put what I feel on paper and am afraid I can't do it. My cup of happiness is so full, and yet I realize that everything is not rosy. You are working so hard, Bobe's sick, money worries, the terrible condition of the world, but, Mother, just look about you, and then will realize our luck. You've given us music and I'll always be thankful. When I look back, I consider too the dramatic, dancing, music lessons, bicycles, clothes and anything else a child could ever hope for and receive. You've given us anything at all that was ever in your power. You are right, Mother, there is a G-d, a wonderful G-d. You've shown me that not by words or comparisons, but by actual faith. You have such infinite, implicit faith that brings you through your hard times, troubled as they must be. Daddy has tried to show me by his belief and knowledge. I understood what he tried to tell me (Daddy is a brilliant man), but the trusting belief I wanted, I could never find before. I'm afraid I've let myself go, but I'm glad and I know you'll understand what I'm trying to say. I had to tell you how I felt as you'll understand better than anyone. I can feel how much older I've grown since I've been at school. You've brought me up so perfectly by trusting me and giving me responsibility. In this way I've tried to live up to that trust.

      Lovingly,
      Your loving daughter Meta

 It is also no wonder that girls with such outstanding qualities like Meta became vulnerable to the Brochos (blessings) of the eminent Rabbis and married young.

 During her final college year, a fellow student, Lester Smith, two years her senior, started keeping company with her, leading to an engagement and the setting of a wedding date.

 Like everything else with Fannie, she planned this coming wedding like a community affair.

 For weeks our eight-room apartment was a beehive of activity. Bridesmaids discussing their dress arrangements, the flower girls, the wedding procession, with friends coming and going to watch the progress of the fast-moving events.

 The meal arrangement too had to be different under Fannie's supervision.

 A committee of the sisterhood in the synagogue was put in charge of the supper to be served.

 On a muggy August day some women left to stop at a farm and purchase a large flock of chickens.

They were brought to the synagogue cellar where after their ritual slaughter by the Rabbi, the plucking of the feathers began.

Many immediate neighbors were summoned to help in this immense task, for there were more than sixty chickens to disfeather and clean.

Sunday August the 6th, 1943, the wedding day broke the heat wave record with an over-hundred-degree mark, but in the excitement of the event, no one seemed to complain.

The ceremony in the synagogue was a magnificent sight with the exception that two well-dressed women, thinking they deserved recognition for the help they rendered, joined the procession.

Fannie smiled and said, "It's a happy occasion, let them enjoy themselves."

In the social hall the sumptuous meal was elegantly served, and though the heat was almost unbearable, it did not seem to diminish the appetites, some guests resorting to a second and third serving.

The following month Lester and Meta settled in Hicksville, Long Island, where Lester, being their only child, joined his parents in the drugstore they owned.

As I look back now forty years later, it is difficult for me to realize that Meta is the mother of six children, three of them medical doctors, and the other three professional college graduates.

Indeed most mysterious are the ways of G'd, and how blind are mortals to the revolving cycles of history.

How truly bewitching are at times the wheels of fortune which in reality is not merely a game of chance but an invisibly formulated plan of untold providential grandeur.

WARTIME RATIONING

It was during the war years that commodity rationing was initiated with shoes being one of the items.

Customers were issued coupons for a certain amount of shoes for them and their families.

The storekeeper would deposit those coupons in the bank which would credit him for that amount.

When a retailer bought his requirements at the shoe factories or wholesale jobbers, he could only get as many pairs as the balance of coupons in his possession.

Prosperous shoe merchants, whose accounts the bank valued highly, would bring the envelope with the coupons and the bank teller would not ever count them, merely take their word for the amount it contained.

But it was different with meager accounts, they merely tolerated those such as mine, and the teller would count it carefully just like money deposits.

One manager of a company shoestore told me after the war ended that he sometimes marked double the amount on the envelope without ever being checked.

This gave the prosperous shoe dealers a great advantage and they often favored customers with an extra pair of shoes without coupons, and their buying power in the shoe market was actually so much greater.

But somehow a Divine angel would at times come my way to overcome those stumbling blocks that had so often confronted me.

With my credit ratings in the trade agencies way down, I was fortunate to have many shoe dealers who trusted in my ability to overcome the economic barriers.

There was a personal touch to imbue them with undoubting faith in my integrity and that I was truly deserving of their full support.

One such firm was the Hill Shoe Company. The owner, Mr. Trachtenberg, in 1922 had given me the agency for the famous children's "Kreider" shoes.

When he passed away his two sons continued to treat me not only as a good customer, but also as a loyal friend.

When they met with a terrible accident meeting death in a gruesome cottage fire, their children recognized my special standing in their footwear organization.

A brother-in-law, Mr. Chapman, was also unusually kind to me and whenever there was a close-out to be sold at bargain prices, he would prefer me to have it.

And if none of them would be there when I came on a buying trip, another relative, Mr. Boonshaft, would take care of my needs to make it most profitable for me.

It was during the period of rationing that I arrived there when Mr. Chapman and Mr. Boonshaft were present.

At that time I owed the firm nearly three thousand dollars, and had in mind to buy only about four hundred dollars more as I was reluctant to overstep their benevolent generosity.

Mr. Chapman came over to wait on me and said, "You know what, Ely, I have a real good buy for you."

"It can't be too big of a sale for I already owe you a fortune," I ventured to say.

"Let us worry about that, I would like you to have it because I know you can make a handsome profit on it."

I shook his hand in grateful appreciation and said, "Now let me see what you are so enthused about."

And what he had to offer was almost too fabulous of a buy to even dream about. I actually never had anything of so colossal a value come my way.

One of the best sellers in a family shoestore are children's shoes sizes 8 to misses size 4. Often size 4 could also be sold to ladies wearing a small size.

What he had was thirty-six cases of such oxfords in colors of black and brown, thirty-six pairs to every case, which meant almost thirteen hundred pairs.

They had a thick leather sole and finest quality leather uppers, and sold regularly at wholesale at $1.80 a pair.

I waited for him to quote his sale price and was flabbergasted when he said, "Ely, if you take the lot you can have it for a dollar a pair."

"Why are you doing it for me, I know it's an extraordinary bargain," I asked him.

"There are two reasons," he stated. "First, we are crowded for space and second, we were permitted to buy it without coupons and maybe you could re-sell it on that basis. That we are doing for you as a twenty-five-year customer and friend."

I was almost choked up in tears at such a gesture of generosity and devotion.

As I settled down on the Reading train on my way home, I again repeated the question to myself. "Mr. Chapman, why are you doing it for me?"

But now I heard again an answer, though it was not Mr. Chapman speaking but a heavenly voice whispering. "It is a Divine gift for the nobleness of Fannie and your sanctified ancestors who were so dedicated to the almighty and humanity."

This remarkable incident was the turning point in my economic standing.

Step by step I had an opportunity now to increase my margin of profits and actually began to see the light at the end of the tunnel.

By the end of the war another splash of sunshine flooded my family life.

WAR ENDS—MYRON COMES HOME

Myron, marching with the First Cavalry Division all the way to Tokyo, had many narrow escapes from being felled on the battlefields.

But it all turned out so wonderful with him coming home now without a scratch.

In one of the letters he wrote home he stated, "I felt the angel of heaven will protect me and always be by my side, for I instructed the army to send five dollars of my weekly pay to Zaidie and Bobe (grandfather and grandmother) in New York, and I always saw them praying for me and I know they are holy persons."

On armistice day I stood on the balcony of my home at the corner of Shamokin and Independence Streets, watching the hilarious crowds celebrating this momentous event.

There was singing, dancing, shouting any thoughts coming to mind, with everyone having something to say to release their panting emotions.

I got about five dollars in pennies and frequently threw them in the street with children chasing wildly to catch them, while all the while I was thinking, "Oh gracious god what a miracle, Myron is coming home unhurt."

In the next several years the other children graduated high school and Fannie got busy arranging for their further education.

It was nursing for the girls and medicine for Roland and Forestry School for Myron. And so Cleo was to get her training at Temple University, Philadelphia, Marquita at the Mount Sinai Hospital in Philadelphia and Myron at State College.

It was also in Temple University that Roland enrolled for his premedical course.

The following years, while difficult and trying, proved in a sense most rewarding.

Whenever the girls came home for vacation they were trailed by college boys they were acquainted with.

Once four of them arrived in late July on a Tuesday. Fannie went to the farmers' market, bought gobs of sweet corn on the cob, and they had the time of their life doing justice to that freshly cut delicacy.

Often they would go to the Coney Island lunch and come back with a pervading onion smell that usually lasted for hours.

With Myron an army veteran, Marquita a cadet nurse, and in later years Roland serving as first lieutenant in the air force, Fannie now began devoting much time to the war mothers' organizations.

With the family mostly away and Fannie busy with social and fraternal activities, I decided to write a novel.

The basic story concerned a coal operator's daughter falling in love with a union leader's son.

But I never found the time to perfect it and I still have it in manuscript form titled "When the Sun Stood Still."

Another manuscript I will try sometime to publish is about my experience as a patient in the hospital.

Once in 1940, while on a buying trip to Philadelphia, I got an infected finger.

I went to the Jefferson Hospital clinic where they told me it was complicated by diabetes, which I never knew I had, and they admitted me there where I was confined for about a week.

I took notes daily of what occurred there, the actions of patients and the feeling of fellowship that develops between them.

I wrote the book, which I named "Shadows of Time and Man." I still have it in manuscript form and, god willing, I may yet publish it in time to come.

When Myron returned from the army he did not know truly what profession to choose, or what would really prove to his liking, so he first enrolled in Penn State forestry school. But when he graduated he felt that he had no true desire to pursue it.

He then entered the University of Pennsylvania law school, which was seemingly the right decision as when he graduated he received a medal award presented to him by the then United States Senator Francis D. Myers and the Honorable Justice of the United States Supreme Court Owen Roberts.

In the eventful 1940s decade my other daughter Marquita was also married, as per the brocho of the eminent Rabbis at the age of eighteen, to a pharmacist and she too moved to Long Island to reside there.

Slowly but surely my economic situation began to stabilize itself but the mounting educational expense of the boys and youngest daughter was a telling burden that did not permit me to make much monetary progress.

THE MEDICAL SCHOOL FRUSTRATION

But as I entered the 1950s decade a shocking incident developed that drove me and Fannie to the point of utmost frustration.

My younger son Roland, a brilliant student graduating Shamokin High School with salutatorian honors, entered Temple's pre-medical school to proceed on the medical career which was his youthful, cherished dream.

In order to conclude his pre-medical course in three years instead of the required four years, he enlisted in a Penn State summer term to get those extra credits.

Months after he applied for admission to the Temple Medical School he anxiously waited for his acceptance but had heard nothing about the results.

Several times he went to the university president, Mr. Johnson, and the executive vice-president, Mr. Gladfelder, to inquire as to what was being done about his application, but the answers were seemingly most evasive.

Once he got a hint that they were displeased by Roland's taking his extra credits at Penn State, but he knew that couldn't be the only possible reason for the delay.

Once on a dismal February night Roland and Cleo came home from Philadelphia with a fellow Shamokin student who also had applied and was getting into medical school in the forthcoming opening term.

Nothing was said about the prospects of being admitted until he let them out at our home.

"I am sorry, Roland, to say that I made it. I didn't tell you before because it would have made an unpleasant trip. All I can say, I hope you soon get the same good news, I wish you the best."

Fannie was at a Moose women's auxiliary lodge meeting at the time and was spared this initial shock.

The fact that Roland's marks excelled those of his fellow town student added insult to the injury.

The following week I went to ask the advice of a presiding County Judge who was a longstanding friend of mine.

It was a night on which legend would have had witches dispensing their poisonous brews when I arrived at his tree-lined corner home.

I peered in the window of the lighted front room and it didn't seem to me that he was home.

A wet snow pelted the ground mercilessly with the persistent chilling wind, which prompted me to go in the house.

The amiable Judge's wife greeted me most cordially and bade me make myself comfortable.

"I guess you want to see the Judge," she said. "He is at a bank meeting and should be home shortly."

She placed some fruit and cookies on the coffee table and had gone to answer the telephone when the Judge arrived.

I rose to greet him, heartily shaking hands.

Being a close enough friend to call me by my first name he said, "Ely, I will be with you shortly after I get myself organized."

When he came back he moved a chair near me and asked, "Ely, what's on your mind?"

I related exactly what had transpired and candidly asked him, "How could such a violent injustice prevail without any possible recourse?" I took out of my pocket one of Roland's usual school report cards with nothing but "A's" on it to emphasize the grievous wrong being perpetrated.

"Is it possible," I plaintively asked, "that because I do not have the financial means as others do, my son's life will be ruined as he had his heart and mind set since childhood to serve humanity as a doctor?"

I could tell that my just and sincere pleading had its desired effect by his profound mood of thoughtfulness.

After some minutes of silence, he rose, paced the room for a while and said, "Ely, I have a few strings to pull and I will do that without failure tomorrow morning."

I thanked him profusely as I left, assuring him that whatever the results, his efforts would remain priceless to appreciate and remember.

I was trimming the Mount Carmel store's windows the next morning when about noon time the telephone rang and I heard Roland trying to catch his breath and spurting out excitedly, "Daddy! Daddy! I made it! The Temple president Johnson called me to say that he was this morning admitting me to the medical school."

There was a telephone at the building where President Johnson related this thrilling news, but in his excitement, Roland ran four blocks to his rooming house to inform me about this breathtaking news.

Outside it was snowing, sleeting, with howling winds adding to the gloom of the dismal day, but to me it seemed like a brilliant June day, almost as gorgeous as the day I got married, at the realization that Roland's unquenchable ambition to be privileged with a medical career had been assured.

I hastened to call the Judge stating that mortal words failed me to express my feelings and thoughts, but I did tell him this: The Talmud states that there are times when one single extraordinary good deed will earn one everlasting glory in the heavenly world to come, and this applied so gloriously to him.

Jestingly the Judge said, "You know, Ely, it was more than some strings I had to pull. Rather those were massive wire cables that shook up the university officials and probably the board of directors."

How deserving Roland was to earn his medical school admission I realized four years later when we went to attend the graduation ceremonies at the Convention Hall in Philadelphia.

It was a gorgeous June day with its splendor supreme when we arrived there and as we went to the balcony, the ushers distributed the programs of the events to follow.

Every branch of the university's departments had its proper sections at the mezzanine below as we observed the magnificent sights of the graduating doctors, dentists, lawyers, engineers, business students, nurses, teachers and others, now dressed in their impressive gowns and caps, waiting for the priceless diploma they so diligently strived to earn.

Casually Fannie opened the program relating to the medical section and shockingly exclaimed, "Oh my god, Roland valedictorian! Look, Zelical (my nickname), see if I am wishfully dreaming." I opened my program as though hers might be misleading and said, "Who would ever think of a small mining town boy, our son, really topping everyone of those graduates here?"

The school officials had kept that a secret even for Roland.

On the previous night at the medical school festivities, a professor had a few drinks too many and blurted out that Roland had a surprise coming, but for some unexplained reason Roland gave it no thought, so it was also a surprise to him.

The people seated around us noted our glee and soon Fannie became busy telling them his accomplishments.

After the graduation ceremonies, the class went to the Trinity Church on North Broad Street, where the religious services concluded the day's activities, with Roland as valedictorian of his class speaking on the duties and responsibilities awaiting them as doctors.

But for our family, it was shortly to be celebrated with a sumptuous dinner at the nostalgic Shroyer restaurant, on the corner of Fourth and Arch streets.

The glow of its ornate chandeliers cast eloquent auras on this historical dining house, with the portly colored waiters treading softly adding prestige to this dignified place.

On Third and Fourth Streets was the center of the wholesale shoe market, and many of the owners and personnel would often dine there.

So we met quite a few I had dealt with and many rounds of congratulations were soon in order.

It was indeed a day that providence seemed to have hallowed specially for us as a date to revere and remember forever.

SISTER ARRIVING FROM ENGLAND

In 1942 the number of people residing in our home doubled overnight when my sister from Birmingham, England arrived in the United States with her family: two sons and two daughters, her husband remaining in England to liquidate his manufacturing business.

This sister, Simke, was in a class by herself. She was as bright as she was beautiful, as intelligent as she was humble.

Before she married she was in charge of our other herring store in Grodno and this was the stand that provided our family with a generous living standard.

We could actually not expect any income from the store my mother was taking care of.

That store was on a narrow street where both sides had stores with one-door entrances, the average store about twenty feet wide and about seventy-five feet long.

Most of them were butcher shops, the others grocery marts, two herring stores, and a few dairy markets.

Many of those stores were taken care of by women, either widows or those whose husbands were dedicated to religious activities.

My mother's store was also the primary place where children's torn or worn out clothes had their rejuvenation.

The store had no door or window in the rear, with two large armchairs placed against the back wall, their crevices, folds, and space beneath the cushion seats containing all the paraphernalia required for the repairs.

One could find spools of thread in many colors, patches and snips of assorted materials to sew up over worn-out parts.

How important such a patching up meant I learned from my own experiences.

Having no sled to coast down the mountainsides in the winter, I used to practice sliding down while sitting and within days my pants turned to shreds, the snow at times touching my bare buttocks.

Mother did not overlook snips of sharkskin to sew over those vulnerable rear end culprits, and it did make a difference.

Mother even managed to tailor some new garment for the girls, mostly of colorful material which she seemed to favor.

Against the store's side wall were lined up the rounded barrels of herring, their salty liquid permeating the unventilated storeroom confines.

In between her domestic chores in the store she waited on customers, the juice dripping as she carried the herring to weigh it on the scale.

In the summer she would quickly dry her hands with no complications, but it was a different story in the winter.

The only heat to warm herself was a bucket with burning coal where she went from time to time to warm her hands, and their irritated skin soon became chapped and cracking.

How she managed to keep the garments and clothes to repair from ever getting spotted was one of those mysteries my wondering mind could not account for.

The left side of the wall in the front where she often sat down to rest was painted white, and on that wall was always a number of names and figures which changed daily from time to time.

For whatever business she did, most of her profits were loaned out to neighborly storekeepers who would come to borrow for a short time.

Time and again I would hear someone say, "Alte (Alte being her nickname), I must have a half a ruble or a ruble, it will be my life saver." Mother would put her hand in the salt-dripped leather pocket and would gladly give it to that person and then take a piece of charcoal and mark down on the white wall what Minde, Hitke or Yentke and so on owed her.

When my father would come from the synagogue and ask her how business was today, she would usually say that she had some money left for whatever we needed.

Surprisingly there were seldom any losses but it was a revolving system of loans without interest to help her neighbors out.

Some days when there were ample repayments, she and father smiled benignly as if that was a windfall bonanza, all pure profit.

So it was no wonder that we could not expect to derive a livelihood from a store that had a woman with a heart of gold, her business dedicated to humanitarian and charitable purposes.

What a contrast was my sister Simke's mode in operating her store.

The store was in a more modern street, one of three in a neat building patronized by an exclusive clientele.

She had the briny herring barrels wrapped in pink or other colorful crepe paper as though it was delicate candy. Each species of herring she gave individual brand names, one of which I remember well she named "Karalewsky" (the kings). It became a favorite brand for high military officers and city officials who gladly paid more for such a select kind.

Instead of wrapping it in newspapers like others did, she had a special waxed paper that prevented dripping and made an elegant package.

She learned to speak English fluently in her youth and was fluent in Russian literature, able to quote page after page from Pushkin, Lermontov, Chekhov, Dostoevsky and many others.

It was her grace, intelligence and ability that made this store a mecca for the most elite clientele.

She married a man her senior by more than a decade, mainly because he was worldly wise, learned and knowledgeable.

In time they settled in Birmingham, England and during the Second World War experienced much of the agony which Hitler's air force inflicted on the heroic British people.

In 1942 they managed to arrive in the United States and came to Shamokin to reside with us until they could find a suitable place to settle permanently.

But while Simke was busy trying to get a suitable town or city to make their home, Fannie began looking for suitable boys as life partners for the two girls.

She also suggested that the older boy, Hillel, would make a good Rabbi, and the younger son, Aaron, an excellent lawyer.

Within that year the girls married with Hillel enrolling to become a reform Rabbi, and Aaron entering the University of Pennsylvania Law School, later joining the prestigious Delworth law firm in Philadelphia.

Long after my sister, Simke, and her family moved out of Shamokin, I meditated on how mysterious are mankind's genetic eccentricities of life.

The oldest daughter inherited her mother's genial qualities, while the younger daughter had the inclination to pursue the pleasures of life.

As for the boys, the older was religiously inclined and studied theology whenever possible, while the younger was a confirmed agnostic and would pace at times in a solitary room learning Persian, Sanskrit and other Oriental languages.

Having my sister's family reside with us for almost a year gave me a great sense of satisfaction and compensated her in part for the happiness her business ability gave to our families with our advanced standard of living while she took care of the store in Grodno.

THE POSTWAR YEARS

The postwar years remained uneventful with the exception of life's normal surprises that married children bring in the course of time.

But there were also times when momentous incidents occurred that spelled the difference between life or death in the passing of but split seconds.

One of those bizarre episodes took place when Fannie and I went on a business trip to Scranton.

There at 305 Penn Avenue was situated the old established wholesale shoe firm of B. Levy & Sons.

I began dealing with them in 1921 and during my dismal economic decades that firm also extended me credit, not on the basis of R. G. Dunn ratings, but faithfully believing in my ultimate success.

This belief was backed up by trusting me with purchases amounting at times to nearly thirteen thousand dollars.

It was on that memorable March 15th that we drove up in our large Hudson car to pick up nearly four hundred pairs of footwear, sold to me at closeout bargain prices.

I expertly packed the back seat of the car solid, and arranged a certain number of boxes in the front of the car.

Fannie had barely enough space to adjust herself next to my driving seat.

With the rear window blocked by shoes, the only way to observe rear traffic was through the side mirror focused exactly.

We started from Scranton on our way home about four o'clock when a wet snow began to fall.

About the time we got to Shepton Mountain driving became hazardous.

To get traction I kept one side of the wheels on the rim of the pebbled road, but as the storm heightened this method became indeed futile.

There were some coal trucks passing us and we tried to follow them as a guiding target, but they knew these mountainous trails well and we soon lost them from sight.

Night was settling in when a blinding fog enveloped us in its misty shroud. I had to open the driver's side of the window to get any semblance of an idea where we were.

I was now driving by the measured pace of seconds, foot by foot and yard by yard.

I knew one wrong move on the curving turns and we would plunge down the precipitous mountain cliffs, which would spell the end of it all.

Fannie offered to go out, walk in front and step by step lead the way, but even this courageous idea could not be done as her door side was blocked by shoes.

For her to go out it would be through my side, and should a truck happen to pass at that time and strike us, it would mean ultimate disaster.

We were then slowly climbing a mountain when a coal truck struck us in the back, pushing our car front against the guard rails.

Luckily it struck us on the upgrade minimizing the impact, or surely we would have crashed over the mountain precipice to our doom.

The trucker set up flares, stopping traffic and thus preventing further tragedy, and when it was determined that we were in a condition to proceed, he let us trail him to Shenandoah.

From there we slowly made our way by the valley roads and arrived in Shamokin about ten o'clock.

Remarkably we somehow took this momentous incident in stride without getting overly upset by it, as though this was part of the price one has to pay in order to accept life's ever-present challenges.

V

The Million-Dollar Diamond

That life supersedes fiction in many instances is a well-known statement, but I had several occasions to see it as a proven fact, and one of them was the following remarkable episode.

When I opened the Mount Carmel store in 1937, I employed an efficient twenty-year-old clerk, Victoria Dempshock.

She was the daughter of a lifelong miner and remarkably attractive.

She had a knack for tasteful clothes and most of them she made herself. Her madras cottons which she wore for work had a mark of perfection.

For quite some time she had kept company with a boy friend, Leonard Wilkinson Jr., whose father was the general manager of the well-known Bastress Lumber Company.

Several times he proposed marriage, but Victoria wasn't certain if she was prepared to make that fateful step as yet.

One rainy morning when she came to work and began marking prices on a newly received shipment of children's shoes, she unexpectedly said, "Mr. Moskowitz, I have a personal question to ask you."

The benches were crowded with unpacked shoes so she sat

down next to me and stated, "I would like to have your candid opinion as to what you think about Leonard as a future husband."

"To be frank with you, Vic (I called her Vic for short), there is no finer family to my knowledge than the Wilkinsons and the little I know about Leonard is truly most complimentary. He is modest, sincere, even tempered and is the kind of person who I am certain would never abuse you. And as for what destiny has in providential store for you, only the future can tell."

Gratefully thanking me for advice seemingly to her liking, she welcomed it with a hearty handshake just as my brother-in-law David came in on his way to the bank.

He measured us up with a puzzled gaze and I explained that Vicky appreciated my advice on a personal problem she was confronted with.

David then displayed one of his inimitable charming smiles and inquired, "What's new in Shamokin?" His changing the subject made me skeptical that he accepted my explanation.

When he left I remarked to Victoria, "I honestly doubt if he believed a word I said."

Nearly four months had passed since the day she asked my advice when the seemingly timid Leonard demanded a definite decision.

"I know we love each other dearly, only you are reluctant to leave your family and job. Now let's set a wedding date as I will not take no for an answer," he declared.

The following month the blissful event came to pass and shortly they opened in Mount Carmel a corner grocery store which they both took care of.

A year later they sold the store and moved to California, where he started on a small scale in the timber and lumber business he learned generously from his father.

Victoria's sister, who worked in Woolworth's Mount Carmel store, told me several times that Leonard was doing very well and they were very happy.

Many decades had passed when I read in the *Shamokin News*

Item's obituary column that on February 18, 1978, Leonard Wilkinson passed away at the age of sixty-four at his home in Reno, Nevada.

It also related in that obituary that he was a multi-millionaire whose hobby was collecting rare diamonds.

One of such remarkable sparklers he paid over a million dollars for, and he offered it to the Smithsonian Institution in Washington D.C., provided they name it in honor of his beloved wife, Victoria.

The Smithsonian Institution readily agreed and the Victoria Diamond is now forever displayed there for the enjoyment of the visiting multitudes.

Indeed, I thought, life is at times far stranger than fiction. To think of it, a poor miner's daughter, clerking in an ordinary family shoestore, starting with a small corner grocery store for a livelihood after marriage, now has a million-dollar diamond established in her honor and it is probably worth many times as much at the present inflated rates.

Yes, how true it is, I surmised, that life's revolving cycles so mysteriously spin their clairvoyant designs of which legendary fairy tales are so magically woven.

TRAVELING SALESMEN, A BREED IN THEMSELVES

Being in business, one has a distinct opportunity to observe people's actions and reactions in life's complicated highways and byways.

But even more vivid than others are the traveling salesmen whose homes are mostly away from home the greater part of the year.

Their extremes of how to deal with the trade were at times most phenomenal.

Some were bold and daring almost to the point of sheer brashness, while, in contrast, others were modest, reserved and timidly unpretentious.

Between those extremes were the vast majority whose varied natural inclinations were truly extraordinary.

Vividly I recall some who left a lasting impression in my mind, though many of the salesmen and the firms they represented have long passed from the earthly scene.

One was a Mr. Harry Klein, who worked for the Crescent Shoe Company on Duane Street, New York for many decades.

Fast moving, somewhat corpulent and spritely alert, he would rush in the store with a hearty greeting, adding a timely remark to boot.

He expertly carried the bulky sample cases to the rear of the store and lost no time in opening them up for display.

Taking for granted that he was certain to make a sale, he had his order book with its inserted carbon sheets all ready, with an assortment of pens and pencils visible in his vest pockets so that at least one of them would not fail him in marking down the order.

If I happened to be busy at that time, he would pull out from the shelves box after box of shoes that were competitive with his styles, and motion in pantomime to belittle the quality and worth as compared with those of his firm.

When I was ready to give him an order, he would at times point out some styles and confidentially tell me that those were hot numbers and really scarce but would make sure that I got what I needed.

Actually they were slow sellers and I would buy none of them.

Making something seem like a scarce item was a well-known ploy to get rid of a bad lemon.

When I would tell him to mark down twelve pairs of a number, he would flash out from his coat pocket a shaft of orders and show me that my competitors bought them in thirty-six-pair lots.

He probably forgot that he often resorted to such a flashing show to induce a larger order.

On the other extreme I clearly recall the four Hunn brothers whose firm, the Hunn Shoe Company, was headed by the older brother, David.

The brothers resembled to a large extent the outline and profile of George F. Will, the well-known columnist, and seemed more like clergy or scholars than shoe merchants.

Whoever came to sell to me would as a rule first stop to observe my window display, noting what styles I featured and what price range I preferred to deal in at that time.

They would come in gently without any fanfare and ask if it was okay to open the sample cases. When I was ready to look over their line they would say, "Ely, you know best what your trade demands, you do the deciding."

I would have them mark down the styles and numbers of pairs and that was that.

Once in a while they asked me, "Are you sure you didn't overlook this number?" And sometimes they were right, so I added it to the others.

In between those extremes run the usual trend of firm representatives, eager to make a sale and doing their best to earn a well-deserved livelihood.

Being on the road most of the time, coming home usually only on weekends, many were tempted to deviate occasionally from the faithfulness of the prescribed family life.

I often heard the salesmen in the store quietly discussing their plans for the forthcoming night.

Once a middle-aged salesman who was considered a friend of our family saw an attractive part-time clerk in the Shamokin store and asked my brother in Yiddish if the maidel (girl) was considered kosher (meaning vulnerable for a date).

That girl was for many years a domestic in a Jewish household and could talk and understand Jewish quite well.

"Why is that mashugener (crazy man) talking about kosher maidel?" she asked when he left.

"Everyone that is employed in the sample shoestore (the trade name of our store) is one hundred percent kosher, maidels kosher enough even for a Rabbi," she jested.

Fannie was busy in the front of the store writing get-well cards for lonely hospital patients when she heard all the commotion about "kosher."

Thinking that the salesman was looking for somewhere to eat a kosher meal Fannie said, "I didn't know that Friedman has suddenly become so religious," which gave everyone a good hearty laugh.

A special breed of salesman were those representing the Ball Band and B. F. Goodrich rubber companies who dominated the miners' rubber boots trade in the anthracite coal region.

Their advertising on any available space, be it farmers' barns or city buildings, made their product a byword in every regional household.

Conscious of their monopoly and the urgent need of shoe dealers to have their brands in stock, the salesmen felt a sense of superiority and conducted themselves accordingly.

Baired, the Ball Bend salesman, was driven by a colored chauffeur, and to a lesser extent this also applied to Mr. Lighthouser of the Goodrich company.

In later years they began meeting a semblance of competitive resistance from La Cross Rubber Company in Wisconsin, also Firestone and a few others.

Once Mr. Forman, a young dynamic salesman for Firestone, spent hours convincing me that his brand could prove an outstanding success if I only tried it.

And to induce me to give him an order, he offered me thirty cases of lace boots at one-third off their marked price, applying it to their advertising allotment.

And what's more, he pounded violently his bare hands on my wrapping counter so that everyone in the store could hear that Firestone guaranteed not only first quality but also seconds.

I bought the lot and they proved remarkably good, withstanding the corrosive acids of the mines' sulphuric waters.

I was astonished when miners came back asking me for a Firestone pair of rubber boots, which I considered a miracle in the making.

Invariably salesmen used to complain bitterly about several shoe dealers who treated them like worn out rags.

One such callous merchant would wait on an ordinary customer while his clerks stood idle, thus depriving the salesman of valuable time for keeping up with their day's routine schedule.

On one unbelievable occasion I was told about a salesman waiting quite a while with his sample cases open for display while the owner was busy with some office work, until the salesman noted that the owner wasn't there anymore. He asked a clerk of his whereabouts. Shockingly, he was told that the owner had left for a merchants' luncheon at a local hotel.

I thought such a cruelty was just a martyr's vision in a despondent salesman's mind until I learned from others that they had experienced the same traumatic action.

Curiously, this sadistically minded shoe dealer was equally ruthless in his cut-throat competition, selling miners' boots below factory price, displaying the price usually on a long pole by the store's entrance, to the chagrin of those shoe dealers who could not afford such a loss.

Salesmen also often complained about certain retailers who would cash their personal check and then go around inquiring about their credibility, and if a check would by some chance happen to bounce back, the news spread like wildfire though either the salesman or his firm soon made it good.

These are but a few tales taken out at random as an example of the fathomless intricacies and traits of mankind's erratic nature, which to a certain extent every human being in his or her own way is more or less subjected to.

THE NIGHT THE DEMONS FEARED

It was during the Fifties that this fateful episode confronted me with its shocking terror.

On an early Sunday morning, I, Fannie, our two sons and a daughter left Shamokin for a day's visit to my two daughters in Long Island.

We arrived there about eleven o'clock and prepared to return home that evening as I had to open the Mount Carmel store and Fannie that of Shamokin.

It started to rain about four o'clock so we decided to leave about five, a little earlier than we planned.

Be careful driving, the daughters warned us in their usual anxiety when we drove back home.

Things did not seem too complicated until we got to Easton. There the steady rain turned into a downpour and we drove slowly into the lengthening line of moving vehicles which found visibility approaching the zero mark.

Slowly we probed our way to Tamaqua and then into the foothills of the mountainous curving roads leading to Mahanoy City.

By now it had became virtually a miniature hurricane with gale-force winds driving the perpendicular sheets of rain against the cars' saturated windowpanes.

Near Hometown and Lakewood Park, there runs the main Reading Railroad lines over which Route 61 makes a complete sharp turn to the left.

It was there that we missed that road crossing, plunging squarely on the railroad tracks.

Fannie, who was sitting in the front, lurched forward to strike the shattered windshield, while all of us were badly shaken up.

The crashing sounds were heard at a bar and inn on a nearby hill, with many rushing down to help us get the car off the tracks.

They could not have come any sooner, for from the desolate distance were heard the wailing blast of a thundering freight train bearing down on the crossing.

In the traumatic shock, the drenching flood of the downpour was hardly felt as we all thanked a merciful almighty for the miracle of having minutes to spare us from a horrible death.

Even in times of seeming disaster there is often a measure of good tidings, for the car engine remained in working order and the tires did not slash as they stroked the sharp steel rails.

We huddled back in the car and, unmindful of the drenching rain striking the broken windshield with full force, we managed to reach the Ashland State Hospital where Fannie was admitted for possible brain concussion.

It was past two o'clock when we arrived home, with every ounce of strength thoroughly drained, truly mentally and physically exhausted, soaking wet as if we had been rescued from drowning.

I had lain down in my dripping clothes on the bed when the telephone rang informing me that my Mount Carmel store was on fire.

If I ever felt as though the world had come to an end and nothing really mattered any more, that was truly the time for such a blackout.

But there is an old saying that "a person is at times weaker than straw, yet at other times, stronger than iron."

Fortunately in this critical moment I did not find myself wanting.

I went to the telephone, called Bob Moyer, the night attendant at the Buick garage where I kept my car, and explained to him my trying situation.

Being as my car was not in a condition to drive, he volunteered to take me in his car up to Mount Carmel.

When I arrived there I noted that they had the situation under control.

The police and fire chiefs explained to me that the center beam in the store, the main building support holding up the second floor, had caught fire from defective wiring.

Fearing a powerful draft would doom this antiquated wooden building to total destruction, the firemen kept the front door closed, fighting the conflagration from a nearby side entrance.

When they put out the fire about four o'clock, the damage was limited to the immediate confines of the store and shoe stock.

My youngest daughter, Cleo, and I remained in the store, thanking the almighty for preventing total disaster.

For the next several days we got busy and gathered the damaged footwear, and within a few days were able to conduct a fire sale.

Luckily too the store had been renovated and made suitable for conducting business, for there were no available store rooms to rent then, and losing this outlet would surely mean a critical setback in my financial recovery.

These momentous and crucial moments of my life were another of those cliff hangers where split seconds meant the difference between to be or not to be.

In the annals of my diary I refer to that terrifying episode as a night when even the demons feared to tread.

MERCHANTS' COMPETITION

In the beginning of the twentieth century Jewish immigration increased steadily in the anthracite coal region of Pennsylvania.

Very few immigrants had ample funds to invest and often started business on shoe-string assets.

Many opened small corner groceries in various sections of the communities they resided in.

Others would venture to open stores on the main streets.

More often than not it was a difficult task, for they were mostly young people in the process of raising a family with all the complications that that entailed.

It was also a time when no government agencies were there to advise and support, and what you earned was what you had.

Under such conditions the dollar one possessed was doubly precious and the lure to succeed often became a compulsive obsession.

No wonder that under such compelling circumstances reasonable people would at times resort to the most deplorable acts.

To relate a few of such incidents, I recall the episode when two merchants, on a main street in Shenandoah, competed fiercely with each other for the available business.

They dealt in the same line of men's dress and working clothes and all that usually goes with it.

In the course of time one of them noticed that he was constantly missing a certain amount of merchandise from his stock.

This being a family-run store eliminated the possibility of a clerk's pilfering job.

On the doors they installed a double lock which actually made it impossible for anyone ever to enter the store after business hours.

Those frustrating shortages began to drive them crazy and they decided to place someone in the store nightly to wait for possible developments.

After many days he heard a commotion in the store's basement.

Holding his breath he detected sounds, and from a peep hole watched the competitor remove a camouflaged opening in the cellar wall that separated the two stores.

Caught red-handed, he was arrested in the process of robbery and his incredible thievery was the regional sensation for years to come.

Such inconceivable cut-throat competition was not confined merely to strangers, but occasionally to members of one family.

I clearly remember when someone was about to buy the building where he conducted his business when his brother stealthily tried to outbid him to buy it for himself, which led to an estrangement that surely robbed them both of peace of mind.

Even more fantastic was the case of three brothers who dealt in the same line of merchandise in a growing coal-mine community.

The brothers would slash prices on many items below the wholesale cost and, stranger yet, they seemed to relish the friction that led to life-long animosity and their degraded standing in their community.

To a lesser extent I experienced the torment of unfair competition from a next-door shoe merchant who, being quite prosperous, took advantage of it to undersell me on many staple items.

One such number were men's and boy's "cloud uppers," shoes with iron cleats on the tips and heels which he would sell below factory cost.

Furthermore he would place a loudspeaker at the store entrance, the sound of which was heard for many blocks around, which proclaimed that every item in the store was sold below the price of any Shamokin merchant.

But in the course of years perseverance and patience were the time-tested remedies which enabled me to outlast the constant difficulties of life's treacherous trails.

AUCTIONEERS ON THE GO

Every store accumulates in the course of years a certain amount of footwear that has become outdated, or too many shoes of one size that would take years to sell out.

This was especially true if one bought shoes in case lots in order to get a bargain price.

In ladies' shoes, sizes 6½ to 9 would move out fast, but sizes 4½ to 6 would prove slow sellers and accumulated in ever greater numbers. In men's shoes too, small sizes and extra large sizes remained on the shelves for a long time.

What was true in footwear proved equally true in every other line of general merchandise.

Quite often auctioneers would visit the regional stores and closeout those lots a merchant was anxious to get rid of.

If an auctioneer would make an offer which the merchant would consider ridiculous, he had an option to wait for the next one to come around.

But if he thought of doing better with the second or third, he was greatly mistaken.

For the auctioneers were a close-knit organization. One would tell another about who was anxious to sell and no one would improve on the first offer.

My first personal experience with auctioneers was when I liquidated my Shamokin street small dry-goods store in 1923.

I sold one lot of cotton fabrics to a Mr. Salkov.

While he was moving it, I asked him to resell to me a few yards for my personal use, and was astonished at the price he was going to charge me.

"At that rate, I gave you the merchandise as a present," I admonished him.

"This is how auctioneers hack out a tough livelihood," he said.

"Don't you have a conscience to make an exception with a seller who gave you an opportunity to make an extra dollar?" I asked him. This happened on a Friday and Fannie had planned to invite him for a Sabbath Eve meal, but she now changed her mind.

This was one instance when being greedy had its deserving retribution.

The auctioneers' auctions had their more exciting moments when the occasion was a Sheriff's or a Constable's sale.

To get the stock at the lowest price possible, they would pay off expected bidders with a certain amount of cash and promise to resell them whatever goods they could use.

At one of those sales on a Market Street shoe store, I had the intention to bid on the stock of nearly 700 pairs of shoes.

I then went to a quiet corner in the storeroom and started counting how much ready cash I had with me to make the usual ten percent initial deposit.

Instantly a Mr. Pivovar came over to ask me if I was interested in bidding on the stock. He was soon joined by a Mr. Fleishman who advised me that we could save ourselves some trouble by a little sensible cooperation.

Making certain that no one observed them, they handed me a hundred dollars in five-dollar bills (A hundred dollars seemed so much more in smaller denominations) and promised to sell me whatever shoes I was interested in most when they got possession of them.

It sounded fair enough to me so I agreed on the proposition.

Soon a Mount Carmel general merchandise dealer, Mr. Sam Spector, arrived on the scene.

Seeing him, Mr. Fleishman exclaimed, "Oi gewald (meaning it's murder) the mamzer (S.O.B.) finally showed up."

Mr. Spector, a neat dresser though he had to contend with a modest pot-belly bulge, headed directly to Mr. Fendricks, the constable, whose walrus mustache and googly-eyed look made him a regional celebrity.

They greeted each other cordially to the consternation of the disgruntled auctioneers.

It did not take long and they met with Mr. Spector to make a payoff to this regular spoiler.

But unlike most other times, this sale took an unexpected and disappointing turn.

For when the bidding started with a five-hundred dollar offer from the auctioneers, a bulky Dutchman with an innocent baby-face look raised his ten fingers, both hands, to double the amount instantly to a thousand.

"That mamzer (S.O.B.) is a killer," said Pivovar in disgust. "What's our limit?" asked the third auctioneer, Mr. Edelstein. They all agreed on a limit of between thirteen and possibly fourteen hundred dollars.

Things moved like a prairie fire now and before long Fendrick slowly counted, "First, second, third! Sold for sixteen hundred dollars to that gentleman!"

The auctioneers left while I went over to the Dutchman to ask if he could sell me the men's kid dress shoes. "Ya, ya gevis" (sure). "I was induced to bid on the stock on account of the Wolverine work shoes I always bought in this store," he said. "Now I may open a small general store at my Dalmatia farm," he explained.

A FORTUNE AN AUCTIONEER MISSED

Around the year 1910 a young man arrived in Shamokin from Latvia, Russia and opened a small store of ladies' wear and accessories.

Stout and of ordinary height, he dressed most conservatively, walking somewhat stooped and slow, eyes gazing downward.

He was a confirmed bachelor and introvert by nature. Religion seemed not to have meant much for him, for he did not even dignify it by being an atheist or agnostic, just merely a total blank.

But he was a proficient merchant and steadily succeeded in accumulating greater material assets.

He lived in a small apartment where he prepared his own meals, with most of his recreation consisting of a car ride by himself or a slow evening walk.

His high-ceilinged store was spacious and filled with costly merchandise worth a fortune.

During the postwar years, ladies' pure silk stockings sold as high as eight dollars and he had them by the thousands. The same was true of other silk dresses and undergarments.

In 1929 he suddenly felt the painful sting of an adverse loss from the crash of the stock market and the drop in silk prices.

Accumulating ever greater material wealth was his life's ambition and this setback had a telling effect on his health.

One Wednesday afternoon, when the stores in Shamokin close at twelve, I passed by his store just as he was standing at the doorway.

His features seemed a bit swollen, his face ashen grey.

I asked him if he didn't feel well and he told me that he was doctoring himself for some ailments.

For the following several years he was often hospitalized and, with strangers taking care of the store at times, it soon became a losing proposition, and when he passed away it was totally different from its former prosperous past.

I happened to pass by the funeral parlor on Liberty Street where two congregation members prepared him ritually for burial.

They saw me coming and asked me if I could help them hold his body up while Mr. Farrow, the funeral director, poured water to wash him.

Swollen to twice its size, the heavy body kept sliding on the wet floor. It was a gruesome sight that kept me awake for many weeks after.

The estate executors sold the store in auction and, as usual, the group of Philadelphia auctioneers manipulated things so they purchased the immense stock for a giveaway price.

Mr. Miller, the main auctioneer in charge of the deal, moved the stock to Bolen's auction house, Market Street, Philadelphia, where it was resold to dealers for nearly twenty-five thousand dollars.

Months later I met Miller in Shamokin, who said, "You know, Ely, I made the greatest mistake in my life by not remaining in the store and getting into the retail business.

"If it brought twenty-five thousand dollars on cutthroat auction prices, think of it how much I could have realized by steady, orderly sales. It could have made me a rich man," he added.

On the gravestone of this unmarried bachelor is inscribed his name and date of birth and death. No one ever visits or sheds a tear at his grave, now as forsaken as the abandoned bootleg coal mines looming on a nearby hill.

And to my mind came the biblical quotation, "Not on bread alone does a human subsist." Indeed how truly this sad episode proved that.

A MAN WHOSE FORTUNE STRANGERS INHERITED

In the last story I related how a person's hard-earned fortune dissipated into mere nothingness, and in this episode it is a tale about a fortune that eventually found itself uprooted from its founder's possession.

The young man in this story arrived in Shamokin in the early part of the twentieth century and began peddling some religious pictures and statues to earn a livelihood.

In time he opened a store in which he now featured a basic line of furniture.

He made gradual progress with substantial savings in his banking account.

During the post-First-World-War years the automobile industry expanded by leaps and bounds with Detroit becoming the center of its activities.

It was at that time that a friend of this man by the name of Oscar Latt advised him about an opportunity to buy, at a bargain price, some ground on Woodland Avenue.

Shortly afterward he purchased there valuable lots on which were later erected Woolworth's and McCrory's department stores, and which enriched him beyond his wildest dreams.

He was happily married to a lovely and devoted wife, but their fondest hope of having children and raising a family did not materialize, which had its telling effect on them.

Short and on the lean side, he possessed a most serious posture with an inquisitive gaze that almost aimed to read a person's mind.

He was learned in Jewish studies and had a scholarly look to justify his knowledge.

Regardless of his substantial wealth, he was most frugal in his living standard and his life's pleasures consisted usually of a car ride in the countryside, short walks and reading.

I began to know him a bit more intimately when, during my financial reverses, he occasionally loaned me some money.

He once asked me if I would like to visit him on Sundays for a chat and get-together.

Because he too had studied in Yeshivahs (Talmudic schools) in his youth, we truly had much in common to converse about, but as it deprived me of spending much-deserved time with my family, I managed somehow to get along without his loans and also fewer visitations.

With his inborn pessimistic inclinations he drifted ever more into an irreversible melancholic frame of mind.

In 1940 his physical condition deteriorated and he entered a Philadelphia hospital for a routine checkup.

It proved to be the beginning of a prolonged illness from which he never recovered.

When he passed away, having no children, his wife remained the sole inheritor of his extensive estate and soon gave up her home in Shamokin, moving to Florida.

While there, she met a businessman and in due time their companionship led to marriage.

Though she was accustomed to a life of frugality, it did not take long for her to change to his mode of a more elegant way of living.

But destiny so often has a way of stopping and making a complete turn-about, so like her first husband, she too began falling ill, drifting steadily on a road of no return. When she passed away it was rumored that much of that estate was shared by strangers so totally unknown to her husband.

Thoughtfully I then surmised how elusive and fickle is a mortal's fate.

I envisioned my friend arriving in the United States, dreaming about the start of a new beginning in life. In time his hopes were fulfilled beyond his wildest expectations, but it seemed his natural pessimistic inclination pushed him into a melancholic quagmire and, having no children, undoubtedly helped to rob him of life's happiness.

But hardly did he ever give a semblance of thought to the possibility of such an ending.

Somehow I then recalled the quotation in the Biblical book of Ecclesiastes stating, "How man of wisdom, skill and knowledge may at times lack the foresight in the possibility of others inheriting the fruits of their lifetime's accomplishments and labor."

VI

The Cavalcade of Blooming and Fading Communities

During the late nineteenth and early twentieth centuries, the Jewish immigrants who settled in the manifold coalfield communities began forming religious and social congregations.

As their number increased, many magnificent synagogues were erected.

With the members coming from different European countries, the amalgamations took different forms in these establishments.

For some unexplainable reasons, those arriving from Austrian Galicia were somewhat antagonistic as a rule to those of Latvia and Lithuania and vice versa.

Often there was friction as to who was to lead in synagogue prayers as a cantor.

At times a commotion erupted when the one leading the prayers on the pulpit would either add a hymn to or, in contrast, omit a hymn from the worshipping volume.

For the high holidays, more experienced cantors were hired to conduct the elaborate services, and their Hebrew and Yiddish dialect and mode of expression played an important part in selecting them for that important task.

The same held true in voting on a Rabbi. Such meetings often led to stormy scenes.

For the Rabbi or reverend was also the children's Hebrew teacher, and his manner of expression and personality and attitude were of special concern to the members.

Many unfortunate incidents and episodes took place when the membership dues were determined by the congregation.

Some members were not in a condition to pay that amount and often it resulted that their children would not be permitted to attend Cheder (Hebrew school), which at best was the wrong thing to do.

As an example I will relate the following case history.

The family had five children: three girls and two boys. The father was a painter whose lungs were affected by the paint's emitting vapors and he could only work part time.

For some reason they rated his dues above the minimum charge, which he could not possibly pay unless he deprived his family of their basic food.

The education committee stopped the children's Cheder admission, which I considered a rank injustice.

I was then president and I personally led his son and daughter to Cheder and told the Rabbi that at no time should he take orders from anyone on the education committee since I took full responsibility for the consequences.

In years to come, the family moved away to Detroit and the son I led to Cheder took up a military career. He rose high in that branch of service, married well with two of his children graduating as medical doctors.

Today he is a leader in his community and equally active in Jewish affairs.

Every year before Rosh Hashono (New Year's), he sends me a contribution for the Shamokin synagogue, often reminding me of how priceless he considers the Jewish education, which thanks to me, was made possible for him.

KOSHER BUTCHER SHOPS

In the early decades of the twentieth century when the dietary traditions of kosher food were generally ahdered to, a kosher butcher shop in a community was almost indispensable.

While it was no problem in the larger cities with ample customers to support such a business, it remained quite troublesome in the smaller communities.

The congregation would provide the butcher with a ritual slaughterer for which he usually contributed a certain amount to the congregation's meager treasury, but often poor business prevented the butcher from living up to his obligations, and frequently meetings were held about what action to take, often leading to friction with a community divided against itself.

But in general the butcher shop became, in those nostalgic years, an institution which formed an important part in the congregation's membership's lives.

It was mostly on Saturday nights, more than any other time, that it became a mecca of gourmet activities and with it a social get-together.

The Shamokin stores were customarily closed at nine o'clock and the end of a usually hectic business day meant an idle Sunday ahead and a deserving change of pace.

Many would get busy with their usual social activities, living it up, but it was the gathering at the butcher shop that proved a most enjoyable and exciting event.

Fresh delicatessen shipments from New York, Philadelphia or Baltimore looked especially good on Saturday nights when the aroma of freshly cooked corned beef and hot pastrami whetted and excited the appetite of the most fastidious epicurean.

Young and old waited impatiently for their turn to partake in this festive delicacy.

The hurrying butcher, his wife, and sometimes an older child were busy slicing the steaming corned beef, preparing bulky sandwiches with Levy's Jewish rye, with the multitude losing no time devouring their tasty assortments.

Others would buy hot dogs, salami, baloney, white fish, herring and other delicatessen items to take home.

Often the telephone would ring to remind someone not to forget this and that and the excitement heightened.

It was also a night when one would get an insight into the latest news, personal or impersonal, and fill others in on gossip that frequently made its usual rounds.

Indeed those were nights that many gleefully anticipated each weekend.

THE RISE AND DECLINE

Those were exciting decades when Jewish families steadily increased and the congregation membership continually enlarged.

Those were also times when numerous Shamokin youths were studying in metropolitan universities and colleges.

Before the holidays, scores of those students would return home for short family reunions.

At the Reading and Pennsylvania Railroad stations, parents and friends crowded the platforms waiting to greet them when they arrived.

Such captivating scenes repeated themselves on the days the students would return to their respective schools.

It was indeed a magnificent sight to envision youth on the move with ideas and ideals, nourishing their hopes for a rewarding future that would enrich their lives.

It is difficult to realize how quickly those years passed by.

Many of the elderly generations in the course of time went the way of all flesh, others moved away. No newcomers arrived and the declining membership in the synagogue truly told of a community on the decline.

Those families that remained were mostly middle-aged or elderly, just husbands and wives or single people.

The graduated children, envisioning no future in the coal region where the economic conditions were not encouraging, settled in metropolitan centers where the prospects of succeeding were so much brighter.

On the high holidays, when even agnostics were emotionally moved to attend synagogue services, there were times when extra chairs had to be placed in the aisles to satisfy the overflow.

With the continuously dwindling membership, the numerous empty spaces became more glaringly noticeable every passing year, with no hope of reversing the grievous trend.

In 1952 costly stained glass windows replaced the ordinary panes and when the golden sun rays tinctured them with their magical reflections it became a symphony of fantastic hues with the eternal light casting so harmoniously its hallowed glow.

In this newly prevailing emptiness the numerous memorial tablets and remembrances on window inscriptions dominated the scene telling a tale of times and days that, like the departed members of those golden years, are gone now.

So sadly fascinating but almost seemingly unreal.

Down in the spacious social rooms with their modern kitchen, the cupboards are stacked with costly dishes for dairy and meat, untold rows of shimmering glasses abound, and there is silverware galore.

But there are no weddings, births or Bar Mitzvas, and seldom any other social get-togethers to disturb the orderly setup.

What a story it tells of eight decades in the rise and fall of the flourishing Jewish coal-region communities.

What glorious accomplishments it can proudly proclaim. It is sufficient to say that in Shamokin more than forty Jewish youths served in the U.S. Armed Forces with two of them making the ultimate sacrifice on the altar of the land they loved and cherished.

Sometimes I fantasize that, like the historical Touro synagogue in Newport, Rhode Island, which became active again after fifty years of isolation, Shamokin too may yet see this miracle come to pass.

SHOESHINE PARLORS

The passing decades have left their distinct imprint on many nostalgic habits, customs and ways of life, some meaningful and some not so truly tolerable.

But about one customary event there can be no argument that it added a measure of dignified quality to life.

That was the then usual presence of shoeshine and hat cleaning parlors in every community of any reasonable size and population.

It was a time where every nationality specialized to a certain extent in various trades and professions: Italians in shoemaking, Jews in tailoring, Irish in construction, cafes and politics, Dutch in farming, Ukrainians in grocery stores and so on.

Those shoeshine and hat cleaning parlors were dominated by Greeks as were restaurants, lunchrooms and some gambling.

The shoeshine trade was most prominent on busy corner stands, encased in window partitions so they could be used in winter and on stormy days.

Activities were usually normal during the week, but come Saturdays, people often had to wait in line for their turn.

Miners who toiled all week in the depths of the mountain fastnesses to earn a livelihood took a special pride in dressing up and attending church on Sundays.

There was a time when I sold the finest quality of men's calfskin shoes manufactured by Endicott Johnson at $4.95 a pair and a miner buying it would ask me if it would take a spit-mirror shine.

It seemed especially meaningful to a youth planning a prospective date.

With the exception of the intolerable winter months, the main streets on Sundays were filled with leisurely strollers, retracing their steps up and down the crowded sidewalks, showing off in their dressed up fineries.

On holidays and especially on Palm and Easter Sundays, it became virtually an endless parade in which the strolling multitudes were eager to display their new clothes, proud to draw some deserving attention.

There was not a hatless man in sight and some decades it also held true with the ladies.

The styles for men were almost standard but each one had a knack of making a little bend or angle more suitable to his features.

As in every mode of life there are extremes and many in between them. The same held true in the shoeshine parlors.

On the corner of Oak and Fourth Streets in Mount Carmel, the middle-aged Greek owner was slender and partly bald. Helping him was a somewhat simple son who was unquestionably an expert in making his swishing flannel polishing cloth sing a tune of its own making.

Since they were quite sluggish in English, only token conversations took place, and they acknowledged the five- or ten-cent tips with a smile and bowing head.

In contrast, I recall the shoeshine and hat cleaning shop across from the Reading station on Independence Street, Shamokin.

The proprietors, two brothers named Louis and Nick Volelis, would start a conversation from the moment a person sat down and placed his feet in the brass molds, continuing to the time he left.

If there were a few getting shines, the questions and answers were intermingled and the subject did not really matter, but it was difficult to figure out who said what and how much was really left unsaid.

The most uninteresting place to get a shoe shine was on the

makeshift corners on the side streets where young boys went on their own to earn some money.

One got a shine, paid and went his way.

Yes! Those were days when the miners earned their livelihood with the sweat of their brow and the risk of their lives, but there was a profusion of pride and honor in their bearing which was truly treasured beyond monetary worth.

INCIDENTS OF A BYGONE PAST

Meditating at times on transpiring events in the decades when immigration was at its height, I recall curious incidents taking place.

One such odd episode occurred in the 1920s when a Jewish shoemaker suddenly left his family, departing without anyone knowing where he went.

Middle-aged and of average dimensions, he had a profile that bordered on the saintly.

Being religious he did not work on Saturdays. The workshop had taken up a corner of his home next to which was a living room, dining room and kitchen with an open porch in the rear. Upstairs were the bedrooms, just ample enough for himself, his wife and five daughters, the oldest about twelve.

On Friday nights, by the sanctified gleam of the lighted Sabbath candles, he would devotedly learn the portion of the Bible that is usually recited in the Synagogue at the Saturday morning services.

At one time he tried to learn how to become a ritual slaughterer and get a rabbinical certification to practice it because he suspected that those performing it did not live up perfectly to the prescribed laws.

One day a tall, dignified Jewish man dressed modestly stopped at his place and asked if he could recommend to him a reliable jeweler.

The shoemaker gave him a certain name and then inquired what he planned to buy there. "No," he said, "I want to sell him a diamond that forever reminds me of some tragic years."

They then both left the workshop and went to the living room where the man told him a long, heartbreaking story.

He was born and raised in the city of Krakow, Poland. His family was quite wealthy and in time he married a daughter of another well-to-do family.

In due time they opened a flour and feed store which proved quite successful.

Having no children, his wife traveled to many chassidic Rebbes so they could bless her with the birth of a child, but their prayers proved in vain.

Then came the First World War, which impoverished him and their families.

In 1920 he came to the United States with his wife, whom he loved dearly, but misfortune followed him when she became ill, leading to her death.

He then took out a diamond and said, "This is what I gave her at our wedding. I can't bear having it with her gone so I have decided to sell it."

"Why sell it to a jeweler? I will buy it if the price is right," said the shoemaker. They then discussed its real worth and, since he was so nice to him, he said he would be willing to sell it to the shoemaker for less than half the price of five hundred and fifty dollars.

The shoemaker told the man to wait a while as he went to the bank and drew out almost all of his savings, and the deal was made.

The man placed the money carefully in his wallet and said he was leaving for Philadelphia where he might open some business.

The shoemaker went upstairs and put the valuable diamond in a box where he kept his important documents and considered himself now doubly richer since the diamond was worth at least over a thousand dollars.

Some months later he decided to get an estimate of it from the prestigious Jewish jeweler Mr. Aaron Liachowitz.

Meekly he came in, telling him the bargain he had gotten, and asked how much the diamond was worth should he want to sell it. It did not take long for Mr. Liachowitz to inform him that it was worth exactly fifty cents and maybe less if he bought it at Woolworth's.

The traumatic shock undoubtedly unbalanced his mind for, as he reached the corner of Shamokin and Independence Streets, he tried to push in front of an onrushing freight train, with the crossing watchman barely managing to hold him back.

The following morning he left unnoticed on the Pittsburgh express that left Shamokin's Pennsylvania station at 7:45, and for weeks no one knew where he was.

His wife managed to hire an apprentice shoemaker to help as much as he could while she took in boarders to provide for the family needs.

In due time they learned of her husband's whereabouts and his wife asked me to write him a Yiddish letter pleading with him to return home.

Realizing that shock and humiliation had resulted in his irrational deed, I wrote him that as a religious Jew he was forfeiting his standing with the Almighty and that the loss of money was the way he was being divinely tested as to his real devotional sincerity and faith in the Lord.

I must have touched the right chord in his heart and soul, for about two weeks later he returned home to the jubilation of his tormented family.

Trying now in a way to atone for the grievous mistake which brought so much suffering and shame to his family, he enclosed the back porch, placed a bed and some furniture there and dedicated it to provide overnight lodging to transients who had no means to afford a hotel room.

His wife complained to me that it often became plagued with

bedbugs when some lodgers left and she was afraid they would infest the whole house.

"Do you think the bedbugs will be good enough to stay away if I write them a real nice Jewish letter on fumigating paper?" I jestingly asked her.

"I really should not complain," she admitted, "for he takes care of cleaning that room, changing the bedding, and glories in the blessings he gets from the stranded wanderers."

The shoemaker and his wife have long since passed away. The five daughters married well. One husband, Mr. Ribner, became a judge recently in Philadelphia. Whenever some of them come to Shamokin they never fail to visit me or call to express their gratitude for the part I played in reuniting the family.

Indeed it was a remarkable experience, one to cherish and remember.

MINERVA WAS TO CURE PATT

Among my numerous customers, Patt Mcginley ranked as one of the most colorful.

He was a middle-aged-Irishman, slim and muscular with bluish-grey eyes that spoke a language of their own.

He was the proud father of two sons who he claimed were a spitting image of himself, though it was only true to some extent.

Like their dad they had worked in the regional mines ever since their youth and lived in a coal company house in a mining patch they rented for eight dollars a month.

In the 1940s the regional mines began closing one by one, and when the boys lost their jobs they left for Detroit to be employed in the automobile industry.

Patt remained idle for a while and, when his wife died suddenly from a stroke, he ventured to open a bootleg mining hole with two partners, one Polish and the other Italian.

North Mountain was lined with such precarious mining operations and frequently an alarm would be sounded for accidents taking place.

The Italian partner was an admirer of Verdi's musical compositions and often sang his tuneful melodies, which reverberated at times with the sound of dynamite blasts to loosen the coal and rock formations.

One day on his way home from work Patt stopped at Kelly's Inn for his usual "miner's" (a beer and whiskey), and when he surprisingly called for another one the bartender wondered if it meant trouble or a celebration.

Truly what had happened was that Patt had stepped on a sharp nail that went through the rubber boot, deep into his left foot, and he was in great pain.

That evening his Dutch neighbor called Minerva Hummel, the pow-wow woman, to get Patt back in shape. "If not for Minerva I would have been dead long ago," she told Patt.

Minerva was busy at Benny's Run restoring the health of an ailing child, so she promised to be in the patch the first thing in the morning.

That day I had to deliver some wedding shoes to Patt's other neighbor, to the left of his home, and she asked me to go in and see if Patt needed more than pow-wow quackery to help him.

Patt's house had three rooms downstairs, the kitchen being in the rear, and some rooms uptairs.

I was very anxious to see how the pow-wow procedure was performed, so we quietly went in the house and watched in suspense the weird scene taking place.

On a narrow, partly worn-out couch in the kitchen, Patt lay on his back, head resting on a pillow. On a nearby chair, Minerva had unfolded from a colorful cloth a collection of dried herbs, some yellowish powder, a small vial of snake venom, some balsams and an ornamented rabbit foot.

Patt, visibly in pain, watched her intently as her bulky body bent and waved over his bony frame while she whispered inaudibly.

The coal stove in the kitchen was on full draft, and in the stifling heat Minerva sweated profusely, her perspiration dripping.

Working with systematic and skillful precision she pinpointed her hypnotic gaze at his look, her shafts of moist flat hair dangling with every shifting move.

There was a flitting smile now showing on Patt's tired face, and seemingly his pain had been greatly relieved. Indeed some of the clairvoyant magic seemed to have begun having its desired effect.

I told the neighbor who watched the scene with me that we had better leave as I did not want to start a conversation with Minerva when she left.

We returned as soon as she went away and were greeted by Patt with a hearty top of the morning to you.

The neighbor quickly opened a window to get the permeated body stench and stifling heat ventilated.

When I asked Patt how he felt he said he didn't feel any pain but when I touched his swollen foot he almost got a fainting spell.

The neighbor told Patt that if he needed anything to knock on the wall, and reminded me to see what I could do for Patt as she left.

I got another good look at his foot, which was inflamed with a fiery redness, and asked him who his doctor was.

"I like Doctor Baluta," he quietly replied.

"He will be here today, you have no time to lose." I noted that at one time he felt himself on the sore spot and grimaced as he touched it.

When I got to Shamokin I learned that Doctor Baluta was detained in Excelsior, so I had Doctor Kallaway take his place.

When I called the doctor that evening about Patt's condition, he told me that he had flirted with lockjaw and the terrifying consequences which it entailed, but that he was now out of danger.

One Monday morning Patt came cheerfully into the store with

his customary greeting of "top of the morning to you" and jokingly asked me if I had nail-proof mining boots for him.

"Indeed I have," I assured him. "A good pair of Firestones will do, it's cheaper than Ball Band or Goodrich and what's more, much firmer."

Firestones it would be and to show his loyalty to that new brand, he put them on in the store right then and there.

As I look back at the weird sight of Minerva's clairvoyant performances, I surmised that it was never-ending superstition. Some human beings letting others at times dominate their mind and actions.

POOR ORDERS

With the election of President Roosevelt in 1932 a new era of social and economic justice was initiated to improve the conditions of those in dire need.

But prior to that time it was up to the local political subdivisions and partly the state to help those in economic distress.

The poor boards of Shamokin, Coal Township and the County authorized to take charge of such help would issue allocation slips for a certain definite amount to purchase shoes, clothing, food or any other necessary items the persons or families were in need of.

Known as "poor orders" they would be made out in the name of certain stores where the poor would be directed to make their purchases.

The recipients of such allocation slips could not use them where they were regular customers or in stores they were accustomed to deal with, but only in the business places whose names were on the orders.

Evidently one had to have a political connection to be favored with such lucrative windfall business, and lucrative indeed it was.

It is well understood that regular shoe sales were at times exasperating enough to exhaust a merchant's patience.

One could best visualize it from the satirical cartoon in which a woman customer is surrounded by dozens of shoe styles and asking the bewildered clerk, "Is that all you have to show me?"

Of course there was also the problem of discount pricing, credit and other complications.

In the poor order, the storekeeper had all the advantages. It was up to him to provide the poor with the footwear that he thought would answer the purpose it was intended for. Style, neatness, perfect fit did not matter. If the storekeeper had what was preferred by the recipient, well and good; if not he would have to take the next best thing offered.

For some unaccountable reason, I never realized the enormity of the poor orders issued or why my store name was not on the merchant's list until the following curious incident unexpectedly occurred.

A customer of mine came in with a poor order for three pairs of children's shoes made out for the Eagle Shoe store.

Somehow mistaking Eagle for Ely's (my store name was Ely's Sample Shoe Store), he came to where he always bought his shoes.

Not giving any thought as to what difference it would make where he got it, I provided him with what he required.

When I mailed the poor order for payment I was surprised to have it returned.

There was a comment enclosed that it was made out for the Eagle Shoe Company and I had no right to take care of it, and therefore payment was refused.

Of course I finally got paid for the shoes, but not without the realization that in this prosaic world it is not how much one knows but rather whom you know.

It didn't take long for me to learn the rules and procedures of the political game and whom I had to get acquainted with and how to get started getting those lucrative orders.

Within a short time Ely's Sample Shoe Store began to receive numerous poor orders and I was amazed how many of my customers were their recipients. So many years of wrongly dislocating them were now rectified to the satisfaction of all concerned.

Another puzzle that troubled me for years has now also been clarified. Mr. David Hirsch, the proprietor of the Bootery Shoe Store, would occasionally ask me to sell him some medium-priced children's shoes he got calls for at times. (He sold higher-priced shoes.) I would charge him only ten percent above my cost. When the poor order incident came to pass, I began to realize that he needed that sturdier footwear to fill those orders. I never mentioned it to Mr. Hirsch, but I once thought of surprising him with a frivolous suggestion asking him for an extra commission to compensate me for the bargain prices I sold the shoes to him for.

REGIONAL DOCTORS

The greatest mystery of life is life itself, and its unsolved puzzling riddles vanish without a vestige of a trace behind the curtain of death into the infinite cycle of revolving time.

In a matter of but passing seconds, the elements of life trade places with stalking death whose fathomless divide no human eye could see or spiritually sense in its mystical phenomenon.

It is but therefore natural that a mortal human around whose destined orbit life and death compete for his earthly existence is constantly on the alert for his self-preservation.

No one can see this ever-ongoing struggle more readily than the doctor or, in many respects, the nurses who are entrusted with the responsibility to preserve a mortal's godgiven gift of a treasured life.

Truly, though, it is not only the physical treatment that matters, but also the patients' psychological evaluation as to their ability in trying to help themselves.

Often it is the human mind that can best manipulate and test their weakness and strength, their merits or faults, their ability to perform the impossible or in contrast submit meekly to the inevitable.

In this respect the mere expertise of a specializing doctor was not decisive in my consideration of him, but rather his capability to balance his medical knowledge with that of evaluating his patients' functional minds.

And what was at times also most important was a dedicated personality of devotion, sincerity and keen consideration to those who so trustfully placed their life in his hands.

In the passing of time I had manifold opportunities to get personally acquainted with many physicians and nurses who left a lasting impression.

Of course the most outstanding personality I recall was that of George W. Reese, the director and chief surgeon at the Shamokin State General Hospital.

In my estimation I did not glorify him because he saved the life of Fannie when she seemed beyond human help, but rather I saw he could perform the miracle of saving her because he was superb.

Those were the years when mining was the predominant industry in this anthracite coal region with countless accidents killing, maiming and crippling those unfortunates trapped in the caverns.

The Shamokin State Hospital was the regional rescue station where Doctor Reese was burdened with the responsibility of saving them.

Once he invited me to his home in the hospital's confines and related the agonizing moments he often experienced when he was to decide how to proceed and what implication his actions would have.

The most trying, he said, was to determine if the amputation of a crushed organ was unavoidable, or could it somehow be nurtured by nature's healing powers and be saved?

"That is why I am moved to pray before operating and pleased for the Lord's guidance. Often I wait until the deadly gangrene sets in and lose no time in amputating one or both legs.

"Yet," he smilingly stated, "there have been times where hopeless cases miraculously healed the shattered limbs.

"The most painful moments are when wives, mothers, sisters or close relatives boldly approach and ask, 'Doctor, was it really necessary to amputate that hand, foot and so on?'

"Of course it naturally deeply hurt me to think that, while I knew there was no other way, they doubted that I did my very best, but in time I got accustomed to those stinging remarks—first because my conscience was clear and second because I realized that it was human nature to have difficulty getting accustomed to seeing one near and dear to you permanently a cripple."

That night I wondered, do people realize his heroic performances and the superhuman sacrifices he made in his efforts to help humanity?

For, besides the emergency operations, there were the regular hospital patients to take care of, and often a large part of the day would be devoted to tonsil and appendicitis operations with only Doctor Buczko assisting.

GENERAL PRACTITIONERS

Those were the nostalgic times when making home visits was part of a doctor's daily routine. A dollar charge by day and usually two at night.

To be awakened any time in the middle of the night was no big deal. The only thing the doctor wanted to be certain of was if it was a real emergency. Otherwise he would prescribe a medicine to take care of the situation.

But there were glaring differences in how far some doctors were willing to perform above their godgiven duty, while others would limit their time and efforts to a prescribed routine.

In some leisure moments Doctor Victor Baluta, a short, corpulent physician whose meditative facial features seemed as if he carried the world's burden on his shoulders, would often relate to me some of his experiences when he first started his practice.

I remember a tale about an early evening call to Hickory Swamp mining patch in a Model T Ford car. He could make it one way but had to be returned on a horse-drawn wagon when a sudden storm immobilized his car.

Once he was detained in the coal-run village on a confinement case in a family of eleven children and he rested all night in a room with four others sleeping there.

What the doctor did not tell me, but which I learned later from many of my customers, was that in his practice he did not accept payment from those in dire need, and to some at times he gave money to buy medicine when they were economically at their wit's end.

What was true of Doctor Baluta also held true for Doctor Kallaway and others who went above the Oath of Hypocrates, bringing succor and relief to those they devoted their services to.

There were of course some doctors on the other side of the coin. One doctor had quite a few rooms in his office and would go from one to another patient while they waited there for him to check on their ailments.

Once a lady came down from the examining table and started to dress. "Where are you going?" inquired the doctor.

"I am going home. I like a doctor to give a patient individual attention, and this setup you have I consider mass production."

There was not much said afterward as he left a bit flustered by this unpleasant experience, while she went home.

One of the most upsetting experiences I had with doctors was when a friend of mine was plagued by a rectal itch. He was recommended to a certain professor in Philadelphia whom he visited one day in his luxurious Walnut Street office. After a routine examination the doctor informed him that it was a stubborn case of Pruritus Anus and he must have an operation. The nurse who took care of the payment and the hospital arrangements informed him that a room would be reserved within a few days.

My friend, who was reluctant to be operated on in such a sensitive spot, inquired of the professor if there were other possible means to cure his ailment. "No," he assured him, "an operation is in order." "Will that then resolve my problem?" he asked again. "No, there is no guarantee on any kind of an operation, one must take one's chance," he stated.

Returning home my friend notified the professor to cancel any hospital arrangement and that he would let him know what he planned to do.

The following week he went to Doctor Spencer in Ashland, who gave him an ointment which within a period of one month completely cured him of his torment.

Since then, the slogan within our family circles has been when an operation is recommended, it is best to seek additional medical opinions.

As in every profession, there are those who have their own opinion as to what is right or what is wrong and do not mind sailing against the stream even though it is so much more troublesome. This was the case with several regional doctors who would perform secret abortions.

With one I knew well, I was conviced that it was not to enrich himself but rather a case of confirmed principles. He began this practice when a niece of his got in the family way at the age of fifteen.

In those years such an unwed pregnancy meant untold humiliation, causing unbearable shame to perplexed families.

This was especially true of his family whose high regard in the community was so notable.

He was a doctor who could not tolerate wrong and he gave much due consideration to others who had experienced the same traumatic situation.

If it was right for him it was right for others and since then he has responded to the call for deserving help.

Such stress has also led in time to the death of the Ashland doctor after a fatal abortion operation.

It was on a girl from New York who had been recommended to him and who expired while he was in the process of operating on her. The doctor was vindicated at a jury trial as he proved the cause of her death was a chronic heart condition that she did not disclose to him.

But he was never the same after that ordeal, which caused ailments that led to his premature death.

The present mode and system of medical treatment has advanced to an incomparable degree compared to that of the early twentieth century, but much of the intimate and individual touch that so beautifully prevailed then has unfortunately vanished, probably never to return.

VII

Regional Lawyers

As in all human actions and activities, the pendulum of people runs its gamut to extremes and the same holds true in the law profession.

There are those who will devote their talent and energy in a desire to attain utmost financial success, while in contrast others will make their primary target the pursuit of justice.

Those aiming for enrichment could not care less if they are called to whitewash the devil, while those advocating justice would not accept a wrongful case regardless of the fee offered.

Then there are, of course, the vast majority who reach for the sensible and logical balance.

The first time I needed the services of an attorney was during the year I opened a shoestore in Shamokin in 1921.

One day a miner came to complain that he had worn the rubber boots for only about four months before they started to leak. Not knowing what the usual procedure was, I told him that I would return them to the Ball Band factory and learn what they have to say. He kept on insisting that other storekeepers would, for a one dollar wearing charge, give him another pair.

"In that case you'd never buy a new pair," I stated. This unexpected barb infuriated him and he said, "I am going to have you arrested by the squire."

By the end of the day a stern-looking constable read a warrant for my arrest and said that a hearing would be held at Squire Hancock's office at ten o'clock Friday morning.

The whole thing truly seemed unbelievable and bizarre to me so I went to Ryan & Ryan, Attorneys at Law, to ask what was the next thing for me to do.

"You have to present yourself at the hearing, and of course you need a lawyer to represent you. We will be glad to do so," he stated.

The morning of the hearing I was found guilty as charged, whereupon the lawyer informed the squire that he would take the case to Court.

Before I left I was told that there was a seven dollar and fifty cents lawyer's fee, about a similar amount for the squire's cost, and three dollars mileage for the constable.

When I returned to the store, my clerk wanted to know if my smiling meant good news. "No," I said, "here is the reason I am smiling, for the boots I originally sold to the miner for four dollars have now resulted in the lawyer, squire and constable making a clear profit of about eighteen dollars."

"The miner undoubtedly got his money's worth wearing them four months in sulphuric waters on sharp rocky surfaces, and I will also get the benefit from a ridiculous experience in learning how to proceed should it occur again."

By the clerk's reaction I doubted if he thought such an outcome was worth a smile.

The next attorney I had an opportunity to get acquainted with was the Honorable Fred B. Moser, who was a Northumberland County Judge for some time.

Tall, somewhat stout with a pinkish face that was crowned with a high forehead that so visibly conveyed intelligence and wisdom, it was his expressive eyes that so tellingly denoted brilliance and self-assurance.

During the years of my financial difficulties I frequently needed his advice and regardless of how many clients waited in the ante room for their turn, he would give me undue considered attention.

In the course of time we cultivated a sense of friendship which proved mutually rewarding. If I were to visit his office in the evenings, his secretary, Miss Zimmerman, would schedule me to be the last, saying that the Judge had something of interest to tell me.

Often after advising me on my problems he would leisurely place his feet on the massive oak office table while leaning backward in his swivel chair.

In the reflecting glare of the electrical light, his wing-tipped, highly polished copper-tan Bates shoes were a sight I appreciated in my admiration for quality footwear.

Our topics of conversation were usually of current events and a bit of politics.

Sometimes we forgot the passing of time, for once when he checked his watch, he exclaimed, "Now I will probably be threatened with a divorce!"

Somewhat embarrassed by making so many visits and getting no bill for his services, I once asked him if his secretary forgot about me. "We are holding your charge for a time we may need it most," he jokingly replied.

In due time I did get a bill but it was for a truly insignificant sum.

He was quite a satirical and witty person. Once while conversing about religion, he smilingly asked me did I think an alert and proficient lawyer could in some way outwit the cleverness of heavenly angels on the day of judgment. To which I suggested that it would largely depend on the fairness of the presiding Judge, to which Mr. Moser readily agreed.

When Judge Moser passed away so unexpectedly it was a grievous loss that affected me greatly. For truly he was a rare personality, a unique institution in himself whose loss was really irreplaceable.

There were quite a few attorneys who were also bankers. Some would follow the strict letter of the law, which resulted in many avoidable foreclosures on mortgages and judgment notes, while others were more liberal and were most helpful to those in economic difficulties.

There were also coal operators who were lawyers and bankers. Most of them were largely involved in politics so they could be in a position to influence the proper officials who had most to say about taxing their mines and coal lands.

Such influence mattered even more when the mines began to close and much of the land was sold by the counties for taxes.

One time Mr. Kashner, a man with great knowledge of the mining industry, told me while buying a pair of shoes, "Ely, if you have a couple of thousand dollars that you could spare, you can buy on North Mountain a tract of coal land that will eventually make you rich for life."

Unfortunately I neither had the funds then or knew what to do with the land if I bought it.

With money then at a premium that land was sold eventually for an almost give-away amount at a sheriff's sale for outstanding taxes.

It was but natural that the banker-coal operators took advantage of those opportunities and came in possession of such land. The land owners leased the ground to bootleg hole-miners who would pay them royalty on all coal mined there, and as yet not a dent had been made in the millions of tons of virgin anthracite coal waiting for its owner to mine.

AN UNUSUAL EPISODE

One of the most unusual personalities that I ever met in my life was a person who once came in my Mount Carmel store and asked for a pair of Vici Kid laced shoes.

He was dressed very poorly, his pants were wrinkled and somewhat short as if shrunk in washing, his coat and vest were glossy from long wear, his shirt and tie truly outmoded, his hat was sweated at the band line, while his shoes had wornout heels with several patches roughly sewed in.

This being only the second year since I had opened the store here, I did not know who he was, so I reminded him that Vici Kid shoes were quite expensive.

Solemnly he explained that he did not mind buying them as he made them last a very long time, so it actually amounted to less than pennies a day.

As it happens, I had bought the Vici Kid shoes from the Dutchman who outbidded the auctioneers on the constable sale. Since I had purchased them at a bargain price, I decided to give this poor man the benefit of it.

When I told him that I was selling it to him two dollars below the regular price, he thanked me most appreciatively, and when I packed up his old shoes he humbly remarked that he would save them as a spare for a rainy day.

He no sooner was on the other side of the door when my clerk, Anna Ositko, asked me if I knew who this customer was. "No, I never met him before. He seems to be down and out and I was glad to give him a bargain," I told her.

"Yes, Mr. Moskowitz, this poor man that so pitifully touched you is only worth about four million dollars if he is worth a penny and he is a well-known attorney. His name is Mr. Deppen."

"You have me puzzled, Anna, I can't get the picture of it in my mind, it sounds absolutely incredible," I stated.

"Yes, impossible but true," and she then explained that his father was a wealthy coal mine operator with vast holdings of anthracite coal tracts. "This son of his inherited the greater part of his fortune, but is eccentric and lives pitifully like a poor man."

In the months to come I learned that he was socially active, went out on dates and even got jealous at a hairdresser girlfriend for dating others.

He had a lucrative law practice but could not possibly overcome the mental block of niggardly stinginess.

When he passed away he directed in his will that his fortune of many millions be placed in a trust fund to help needy students in their college education. It stipulated certain rules and conditions concerning smoking habits and other ethical and moral behavior.

The First National Bank of Mount Carmel had been designated to administer this most admirable endowment fund, and I often thought how proper it would have been for the bank to publish a yearly report in the local press so that Mr. Deppen's name could be recalled and remembered in gratitude.

One lonely evening I meditated about the day when this seemingly impoverished man commented that the old trice-patched shoes would come handy as spares for a rainy day while his invested millions kept on enriching him daily.

It then dawned on me that the meaning of fiction is truly yet to be defined and that the vastness of its magical realm is a fantasy not yet envisioned.

THE ATTORNEY IN NEED OF SHOES

While I have published this story in my book "Harvest of Memories and Thoughts," I thought it timely and fitting to relate this remarkable experience in this chapter about regional lawyers.

During the spring of 1977, the eminent journalist Karl A. Hoffman interviewed the Honorable Judge Robert M. Fortney who narrated his remarkable life's story that was published in the May 19 issue of the *News-Item*.

In that memorable interview the Judge told nostalgically about the childhood and adolescent years when he was raised and guided by his devoted grandparents.

After his grandfather passed away, his ambition for a higher education seemed at times to be an insurmountable problem, but his resolute willpower and determination finally culminated in the growing achievement of graduating with a law degree from the Dickenson College Law School.

He began his law clerkship at a salary of $50.00 per month, and as his boss occasionally forgot to pay him on time, he was often left practically penniless.

It was during these trying clerkship years that Judge Fortney experienced an unforgettable episode, and here we quote his exact words in the interview: "I remember vividly that I was obliged during my early clerkship days to make an appearance in Court at Sunbury. I desperately needed a new pair of shoes, with no money in my pocket. I then visited 'Ely's Sample Shoe Store' operated by Fannie Moskowitz, and explained to her my problem. To this day I bless her memory. She gave me a good pair of shoes and refused all my future efforts to repay her kindness. That is one reason that when Fannie's son, Myron, was opposing attorney Peter Krehel as a candidate for County Judge, I welcomed the opportunity to give him my financial and moral support."

Since those memorable yesteryears of his law clerkship, Mr. Fortney has been successfully elected four times as District Attorney of Northumberland County and two times as Judge.

This remarkably moving episode tells a tale of days and times when perseverance and motivation were the incentive to succeed in an era where the guidelines were morality and ethics.

REGIONAL POLITICS

Unlike other professions, where accomplishments can in time be judged by achieving results, the field of politics is different.

A person can be elected several times to a political office without ever being able to fulfill his electioneering promises and yet find sensible excuses why he failed in his efforts.

There is a well-known saying that facts and figures can be juggled to conform with the views of those who wish to distort them. Such contortion of life's realities are even more commonplace in the realm of politics where illusions reaching for the impossible are so much a part of its setup.

There are countless reasons an elected official can give for why his promised actions did not materialize.

That the Federal Government impedes action on the local level is often a reason given; changing circumstances and conditions is another excuse; and that it is not so easy to dislodge entrenched bureaucracy is a well-known complaint. The variations are manifold.

This cavalcade in the political cycle, be it national or local, is part of a system that gravitates ever more swiftly by its own creative power.

So I will refrain from chronicling the political officeholders that I knew as it will only be a repetition of episodes and events, only the names of the persons changing, but I thought it might prove interesting to recall the political system and the party leaders who manipulated the exciting art of political intrigue and skillful maneuvering.

The most important event in local politics was the election of committeemen and women in the county's various precincts and wards, and their election of the chairman.

It was these Republican and Democratic committee chairmen who then became a source of immense power that no one in the county could equal.

It seems as a rule that once a chairman is elected, he is sure to be re-elected many times over again. For during his terms it is his prerogative to dispense patronage, and this is usually placed in families where it counts most.

Besides giving out jobs, there are so many other political favors to grant, such as special consideration at State Hospitals and Institutions, parking privileges, priority in snow removing at home—to mention only a few within their ability to grant.

It is therefore no wonder that the candidates for various political offices look forward most anxiously to close relations with the county chairmen and follow their advice about conducting their own campaigns.

Usually no campaign is lacking in bitter and acrimonious accusations by the rival candidates against each other, as well as by the parties' executive committees, but not many seem to know that while all this rivalry is in full swing, the Republican and Democratic county chairmen occasionally have intimate telephone talks about various problems that emerge in the course of time, and also about the possibility of a trade, dumping certain candidates in order to favor others that would prove more beneficial to them.

It is these trading and dumping accommodations which often cause many vulnerable candidates sleepless nights.

When a decision is agreed upon by the chairmen, sometimes with a cordial toast to seal it, its knowledge soon finds its way by the usual channels of gossip and rumor.

The candidate would never dare to ask bluntly if those rumors are true in fear that he might lose his political standing with the organization in a future election.

I know for a fact that one such candidate for a county office, though he realized that his chances to be elected were reaching the zero mark, redoubled his efforts to beat the odds against him. He took a second mortgage on his home, got as much as he could in loans and contributions from friends and relatives, and even secured a loan from a high-rate interest company. It took him years to get somewhat straightened out, and if not for the children's sake, it would have probably led to a divorce.

The most potent drains on a candidate's monetary resources were advertising, countless billboards and posters on road displays, radio time and loudspeakers cruising around loudly proclaiming his worth, but the most agonizing were the endless visitations of so-called supporters who contended that they had positive control of so many voters but that it required money to show them and their families some favors which they would say came with the compliments of this kindhearted candidate.

I once was in an office where a pleasant-looking man came in and introduced himself to the candidate and stated that he was the secretary of a newly formed social organization, they were having a picnic on Sunday and needed half a barrel of beer to complete the arrangements. "It will mean many votes for you," he assured the candidate. When the candidate offered to call the beer distributor to deliver it to the picnic, the man replied that he would rather have the thirty dollars in case others had also contributed beer. Then he would use it for extra hot dogs. Of course he did not get the cash, and this was one time when a fictitious organization found itself in the place it belonged.

If a candidate preparing for his campaign figured on a certain amount of money to finance it, he was fortunate if the amount had only doubled by the end of the campaign.

So many unexpected extras normally showed up that it amazed him how they escaped his attention.

Some of those unforeseen incidentals included the solicitations of various fraternal, social and religious organizations for a candidate to place ads in souvenir programs or outings announcements during the campaign time.

Actually no candidate would refuse such a bid, so it was truly meaningless as a vote getting proposition since they all took ads, but such additional expenses meant at times the straw that broke the camel's back.

As the election day neared, the average candidate was by now mentally, physically and financially drained to the exhaustion point, but the real test of his political sagacity came on election night when the counting began and the figures were recorded.

All day long the prevailing stillness was like an ominous quiet before an approaching storm, but emotions heightened as the evening hours began to tell the tale of approaching defeat or triumph.

For it was the culmination of strenuous months of hopes, aspirations, prayers, and placing every ounce of effort on the scale of elusive destiny.

If the tide was running decisively against a candidate, he and his family would make peace with the thought of an unavoidable loss, but in contrast it would prove an agonizing ordeal when the figures were close and constantly zigzagged in all directions.

Sometimes the results would not be known until the wee hours of the morning and even not then, and the numbing frustration would reach the breaking point for candidates and their families.

Truly only those who went through such a strenuous experience could really sense its nagging pangs, yet those who usually embarked on the crusading field of politics as a rule possessed the stamina, courage and gameness to take defeat in its stride.

For the record proves that most of them surprisingly found themselves again in the battle line of future election contests.

It is difficult for the average human to understand how a person giving so much time, effort and money, only to find himself a loser, can start such an ordeal all over again, but the fact is that once a candidate is bitten by the political bug, he thrives in the glare of public attention and publicity, and only time and advancing age usually cure such a distinct motivation.

There is one point that people overlook: the usual custom of sending a congratulatory message to the winner.

For so many months the candidates have run the gamut to cast vehement charges against each other, and it has undoubtedly left a bad taste and feeling for each other.

Now one sends the other a congratulation, wishing him the best in a future of success. It is the American way of correctness and fair play, but for a human being possessed of passions and emotions, such a congratulatory climax is undoubtedly a painful ending to a trying campaign. It is also worthwhile to mention that sheer luck plays a great part in the annals of political activity.

Many of our most outstanding presidents were miraculously elected, while quite a few of mediocre rank were voted in by tremendous majorities.

At times one single slogan or deed changed the tide of an election campaign. The famous quotation "Rum, Rome and Romanism" was one of them, while Muskie crying during a speech in New Hampshire put a finishing touch to his candidacy, and Governor Romney's quotation, "I was brain washed on Vietnam," was another error that proved fatal.

But truly what we call luck is really the cycle of providential mysteries which we sometimes instinctively feel, but which is out of a mortal's realm to envision or understand.

EPISODES IN A POLITICAL CAMPAIGN

In 1975 my son Myron was nominated in the primaries as a candidate for judge of Northumberland County, and right after Labor Day I began campaigning for him.

Having been in the shoe business in this region for nearly fifty-five years I was fortunate to have earned the friendship of the customers I dealt with.

It was especially true in the Shamokin store where my illustrious wife, Fannie, was admired in her love for children and generally her affection for people.

Being that Myron graduated from Shamokin High School and was now practicing law in Shamokin, he was very well known in his home town so I thought it advisable to campaign in the smaller mining communities and hamlets where I was so well known.

I would usually leave the house about ten in the morning, place all the campaign literature in the car and return about four o'clock. I made up my mind to cover each community from door to door and street by street, make personal contact whenever possible, or if no one was home, leave in the mailbox or door my campaign literature I had with me.

On the first day, while I began making my rounds in Kulpmont, I saw a husky, middle-aged, burly person coming from across the street directly toward me and he gruffly inquired if I was the one that had removed the opposing candidate's circulars from the slots to put Myron's in.

When I explained that this was my first day out and such tactics were totally abhorrent to me, he grumbled, "Whoever it is they better be prepared for some dire consequences."

Some days later I campaigned in Marion Heights, situated on a north mountain plateau that is always the first to touch the snow clouds as autumn advances. Campaigning there that day was the attractive wife of the candidate for District Attorney with two of her children accompanying her. "When you get to the street above be careful for some vicious dogs," she cautioned me. I thanked her profusely, and indeed it turned up worse than I thought.

I managed to deal somehow with that problem but was not so successful when I visited social clubs and various bars as I followed my routine rounds.

It was there that I usually received a most enthusiastic reception as they lined up for a round in toasting me for success.

Where ordinarily the clientele was satisfied with a medium-priced Kessler or other regular brands, it was now Cutty Sark and beer or other expensive scotch usually reserved for special occasions.

Once a bar was quite crowded and I wondered if my present finances would suffice to cover the prospective charge.

I truly just about made it and as it was nearly three o'clock I decided to call it a day.

As I left with many good wishes following me, a customer of mine followed and quietly stated, "You know why it is so crowded? A committee pep-up meeting working for the election of your son's opponent is going to be held here soon. You came in a lions' den wasting your money," he remarked. But somehow I was not dismayed for, after being involved for more than half a century in civic and political community affairs, I was far from being naive in the facts of life.

One thing I indeed was not short of and that was getting advice on how best to utilize the campaign and what to say and do.

Many would confidentially inform me of some small, nasty things about the opposing candidate. Some somewhat a little bolder would even get in personal details, stating that as a matter of fact they had been known for years. Others would relate some personal experience that I would never think possible.

I often learned that they were not well disposed to Myron and voted in the end against him.

Usually I would change the subject, for from the very day we started campaigning, Myron and I held to the principle that whoever never did any wrong should throw the first stone, and we knew we were indeed but mere mortals and others would have no difficulty finding fault with us.

It was always my contention that no one gains from a negative campaign and as I reasoned with people to vote for Myron I would state that his opponent was surely worthy and deserving the honorable position as a judge, but that Myron might be temperamentally a bit more suited.

Another episode I clearly recollect occurring during the campaign was during my last day of campaigning in Marion Heights.

It was a cold, dreary, autumn, blustery day and, tired from a long day's efforts, I had but one more home to call upon before I called it quits.

The front door was locked so I went by the back yard and was greeted by a fiercely barking dog. An elderly man emerged, ordered the dog to return to his shed and invited me kindly to come in. From the huge Dixon Coal Stove, a glowing warmth filled the humble kitchen, and I gladly accepted his offer to sit down and get the raw autumn chill out of my shivering body.

Shortly after, I stated my usual campaign praises for Myron, but I noticed a glistening tear slowly rolling down his unshaven, wrinkled, ashen-grey face. After some seconds of depressing silence, he quite emotionally unfolded for me the following inspiring story.

"I started as a slate picker in the mines at the age of ten, and worked in the regional collieries ever since, until they practically all closed. One year the Scott Colliery, where I then worked, experienced a prolonged strike. With five children to take care of, my meager savings were quickly gone, and nowhere was there a helping hand to be seen. It was especially heartbreaking when the Christmas Season came around, very, very depressing!" he said.

A spasmodic asthma cough interrupted his tale, and when he caught his breath again he continued.

"My five children insisted that we all go to Shamokin, if only to see the tree illuminations and the exciting store displays for the Christmas Holiday. My wife thought that we could take some of the money saved for food and buy a pair of shoes for the older daughter. A wet snow fell on the day we all came to Shamokin, and as evening descended we all entered Fannie's Shoe Store (they called the sample shoe store Fannie's) to buy that pair of shoes for Olga. It was then that Fannie inquired about the other four children, they all had worn-out shoes. I explained the situation, and that even the pair we would buy would be paid for from necessary table food."

Another spasmodic asthma cough seized him as he gently wiped off the rolling tears from his ashen-grey face. When he caught his breath, again he emotionally continued.

"Fannie called on her clerk to fit them all up. 'No children are going out of this store with no suitable shoes for Christmas,' she said, and would not accept any money, even for the pair we were to pay for. 'Use it for the food you need and pay me little by little when you start working.' So you see voting for your son is the least I can do to repay that memorable golden deed. In fact, it was priceless," he added.

A misty, cold rain mixed with snow greeted me as I left for my car to drive back home, but those memories of Fannie's golden deeds made it a glorious day to remember forever.

VIII

High School Graduations

The twentieth century was just awakening from the nineteenth century doldrums with education assuming its proper place in the nation's life.

It was only a few decades back when boys as young as the age of eight worked in the collieries sorting out the various sizes of anthracite coal in eight- or ten-hour shifts. They were known as red finger youths, the fingers being mostly used in that dreary job.

It was the time when immigrants had to start from scratch when getting married, raising a family and providing a livelihood.

The earnings of a father were quite insufficient to take care of a family, especially if it was numerous, and children went to work at an early age to help out.

Those able to graduate from an elementary school considered themselves fortunate, but most appreciative were those who had an opportunity to enter high school and they felt especially blessed that nothing happened to impede their graduation.

The senior high school year truly began to leave its imprint in students' lives. In the high school book were recorded the students' activities and performances. Those who excelled in sports, the high school band, the debating team and other functions were busy making certain that they got full credit for their meritorious achievements.

Getting the coveted high school ring with its special insignia was another proud moment in their lives.

Students began to share with each other what plans they had for the years to come.

All in all, every new day became more fascinatingly exciting as the glorious graduation day came ever nearer. The great event to come now was the prom dance. It created moments of joy and happiness as well as sometimes sorrow and grief.

Girl students who were certain who was going to ask them as their prom companion were heartbroken when others were chosen, and the whole family would accept it as an unconsolable tragedy that spelled ruination for such a splendid event.

The same held true when a girl refused a boy's invitation and picked a prom companion of her own choosing.

Picking the proper gowns to draw attention was a task of special importance in itself. Time and again a girl would try it on saying, "Sis" or "Mom, What do you say? Tell the truth. You think it does justice to me?" The answer would usually come, "I am getting tired of telling you, you couldn't have picked anything better if you had gotten it at Wanamaker's in New York."

Boys who usually could care less how they dressed wanted to make certain how their formal outfit looked on them. Mom, sister or brother, tired of his questions, would at times exclaim, "Bernie, you are gorgeous, Rudolph Valentino has nothing on you."

What corsage to get was also important. "This one I know she would like," they would usually confidently say.

I know this procedure because I went through these formalities with my children.

When the boys were ready to leave, some would quietly ask Mom for an extra dollar. "I don't want to get embarrassed in a pinch." Mom would usually smilingly oblige, proud of her son getting a high school diploma.

With traditions being firmly imbedded in the immigrating multitudes, the problem of intermarriages was an ever-present concern, and those prom dances were a critical time to worry the parents.

Grandparents especially would feel unnerved as they watched Evelyn taking out Tony, Rebecca going out with Paul, Lillian and Doris with Grant and John. "Nothing good can come out of it," they would complain.

Fannie once told her mother, "What are you worrying about, they are only going out for tonight," but there seemed to be no consolation for grandmother who in annoyance replied, "What a night it may prove to be."

Four of my children played solo musical numbers during graduation ceremonies, with the exception being my son Myron who played a trio, "Three Blind Mice."

A lady sitting next to me remarked that the three graduates indeed did justice to the "Three Blind Mice" number. It must have been good, for she told me she was a music teacher.

High school graduating time was magnificent indeed in more than one way. It was inspiring to observe youth in its full bloom, sparkling with a fragrance so truly invigorating.

In their splendid gowns adorned with the corsages graciously given them by their companions, their flitting stride was a symphony of elegance and grace.

There were gleaming twinkles in their dreamful eyes as if they were wondering what fate had in store for them in the magic of this glorious night forever to remember.

This was June, the splendor of spring in its magnificent bloom, and harmonizing with it were their dreams, hopes, desires and aspirations. But in nature, spring will return in the splendor of rejuvenation. Not so in mortals where its grandeur has but one passing cycle to enrich them.

SUPERMARKETS

There are many who still remember the era when the corner grocery store was the mainstay for replenishing the family needs.

It was usually a man-and-wife business, and they operated it from early morning until late at night.

The store was on the ground floor, including the kitchen and storage room, with the living quarters upstairs.

With the advent of the supermarket, groceries became a tale of the Middle Ages, and it is truly inconceivable that they are really only four decades past, but for myself the supermarkets are not only the apex of comfort and convenience, but also a most propitious place to observe and learn the untold traits of human nature.

Even before I get near the entrance I marvel at the way various persons give proper consideration for their prevailing actions.

People will wheel their shopping carts to where their cars are. Some will leave them right then and there, right in the path of other parking places. Some will move them a bit out of anyone's way, while others will take the time and wheel them back to the platform where they belong.

Entering the fruit and vegetable aisle I find it sometimes blocked by some who have their carts abreast and start a conversation, which is often interrupted by an impatient shopper. At other times they are reminded by bumping their carts and no words are exchanged.

At the meat counter many will take their time to check on the assortment, quality and prices. In the meantime they have their cart placed at a sharp angle, and before long the whole aisle gets in an overcrowded tangle.

While the cart is moving, it at times catches on some stacked merchandise. Some stop to get it in order, others wait for the workers to straighten it out.

It is strange to see how people that could hardly move in their overweight condition get fascinated in the bakery department where strawberry shortcake, richly baked pies and so on find their way in their carts.

One time I saw a girl who had only one item to check out and she asked the woman in front of her who had a big load if she would let her go first as she had a dog in the car and had left the window open by error. "I too have my problems, you will have to wait for your turn," she was unhesitatingly told. By chance another check counter opened and the problem was thus solved.

The most tormenting event while shopping in a supermarket is to see a mother or father trailed by their children and with a limited sum to spend. The children passing the candy and cookie aisles or other aisles keep on picking things up, and the yelling comes back, "Put that thing back, we have no money to buy it."

The scene gets more glaringly painful when in contrast a well-to-do family follows them and the mother keeps saying, "You think, darling, you will like that, my sweetie pie," and they probably get more than they can consume.

Once a woman was caught shoplifting. The manager and the girl were on the store's platform waiting for the police cruiser to pick her up. People who previously were in a hurry to leave suddenly remained where they were, waiting to see the end of the episode.

Seemingly people will somehow find a sense of satisfaction in seeing others in trouble.

The action and reaction of shoppers also finds its counterpart in a store's personnel. Some are stern and impersonal, others are pleasant, parting with a wish, "I hope you have a nice day." Some keep on chatting with the other checkout girls which makes one feel as though they don't know the shopper is anywhere around.

I often thought that, even with the computation system, sooner or later an error will be made.

Some people do not come shopping in cars, and on rainy days they would be approached at times by friends if they need a ride home. At other times they would ask acquaintances if they could give them a ride.

I was astonished to hear a man reply that he lived on the other side of the town. Actually it was only a matter of a few blocks.

There are untold events and episodes to recount as one observes people act and react instinctively to the eccentricities of life that are as mysterious as the very meaning of God's creation.

MY SONS' BAR MITZVAHS

Ingrained indelibly in the depth of my heart are the warnings of many doctors that childbirth might prove fatal to Fannie.

When destiny proved them wrong, the forthcoming privilege of raising a family was a blissful joy to doubly enrich our lives, and as the time neared to celebrate my sons' Bar Mitzvahs, it was indeed a monumental occasion to behold.

Four of our children were born in the autumn (the fifth youngest daughter, Cleo, born in August, missed it by a month) and celebrating the Bar Mitzvah in the golden September and October months meant again something special.

My two sons' birthdays are about three weeks apart, but on rare occasions the Hebrew Lunar calendar results in reading on Saturday the same portion of the Bible and the Haftoro (the prophets' appendage portion).

Here again these festivities became a community affair. Sisterhood and ladies aid groups formed to purchase chickens at the regional farms with the ritual slaughterer taking care of them in his residential backyard.

The scene where the feather-plucking was performed would prove to be a sight for an artist's windfall. Five women were hired to do the job, a few supervising. When this was completed, the messy task of opening and cleaning the insides was expertly done, and when the chicken reached the kitchen, it was a spectacle to admire.

At the Saturday morning services, it seemed like a Rabbinical convention as many relatives and my father's friends were Rabbis and religious leaders.

There were the customary comments and speeches in the hallowed atmosphere of these Bar Mitzvah celebrations, but the highlight of the event was the Bar Mitzvah address, in which my son explained that he fully understood his responsibilities, duties and obligations to his fellow mankind and the gracious almighty.

The speech was also repeated in Yiddish to satisfy the grandparents and the elderly Rabbis who glowed with a halo of glory at the performance of the new generation, the future leaders to come.

But it was the Suddah (party) on Saturday night in the synagogue's social hall that culminated in a magnificent climax. After a sumptuous, enjoyable meal, melodious Hebrew, Yiddish and English songs were rendered by local talent and so were musical arrangements of soft and lyrical tunes.

Folklore dancing and traditional waltzing were a graceful sight. It was equally enjoyed by those who could not participate and were thrilled watching it.

About midnight, when almost everyone had left, the family and many enthusiastic friends who were reluctant to let such a glorious evening pass by started celebrating all over again with a renewed spirit of togetherness in singing and dancing that made this truly a most outstanding red-letter day.

The following Monday I would leave in my Nash Ambassador car for Scranton to pick up some shoes from Levy and Son. In the grandeur of the golden October day, the bewitching crimson foliage on the winding mountain sides was a panoramic vision of heavenly splendor. Its sun-kissed resplendent hues inflamed in a symphony of rare enchantment.

Such was the glorious season in which I was divinely gifted with my cherished family, and I responded to its magical spell as I coasted along in its ravishing magnificence.

Recalling now the transpiring events of the Bar Mitzvah celebrations, I think that the crowning of glory those days was my sons' recital of the prophetic portion of Isaiah that was the appendage to the Torah (Old Testament) Reading.

I have made a free translation of its Hebrew texts which expresses the intended meaning and spirit which it aimed to imply, and because these prophetic chapters carry such an eternal and potent message to mankind for all times to come, and its inspiring words truly are a priceless treasure to cherish forever, I feel privileged and proud to make it part of my book.

ISAIAH, CHAPTERS 42 AND 43

So said God the Almighty, the creator of the universe and the myriads of celestial bodies. The maker of the earth and its reproductive power:

"He who gave a soul to humanity and instilled them with a spirit of progress and action. And in the scheme of things I called on you, Israel, as a promoter of justice. For that I was to strengthen your hand, watch over you and preserve you as a covenant nation to enlighten others in my ways. I have chosen you to open the eyes of the blind, to unlock the chains of the spiritually imprisoned, and to liberate the unenlightened from their darkness of mind.

"It was for you to proclaim the true meaning of my name and to advise that my honor cannot be shared with others or my praise be transferred to the idols. That which has already happened is for all to know, but that which is to be only I can tell. Even before the seed is planted I can forecast its development. You, Israel, were to lead the nations in a new song to God so His praise could be heard to the end of the earth. Those who go down the unchartered lanes of the sea and its tributaries and are marooned on lonely islands shall know me.

"You were to carry the banner of my glory through land and desert, even the unsophisticated of Kador shall sing it, and from the rocky peaks the mountain folks shall shout it, to do honor to God and His praise between nations to be told.

"To help you in your mission the Almighty was to disclose His physical powers, like a mighty warrior He was to proclaim revenge His enemies to overpower.

"It is true I have been silent for so long, but those are my ways from time immemorial, though when I am in anguish I hold back as in the growing pains of birth but only to retribute in the end. And when that time comes, I will devastate mountains and valleys and all their fruitfulness I will destroy; I will turn rivers into islands and lakes I will make dry, and when the world shall have learned its lesson, I will perform the miracle of leading the blind on highways they never traveled on, on pathways unknown to them they will find their way; I will turn for them darkness into light, and most difficult obstacles will disappear.

"Now those are words not only to be said but destined to be fulfilled into action, and then those who erred will hide in shame, those who placed their fate in idols and said to the statue, 'You are my God,' shall bow in humilation.

"In view of all those facts, isn't it provoking that none turned out so totally blind as my own servant nation and so deaf as the very representative designated to fulfill my mission, who proved so blind as the one I thought most competent, and as blind as the chosen of God? Many hardships befell you as a reminder of your mistaken attitude, yet you did not take heed, and what is more, you possess the faculty to understand, yet you would not listen. It is only because God wished to be just in His promises that He will endure you and wait for you to change.

"Yet you are a nation forever persecuted and tortured, your youth are perverted and to escape the reality they turn to unworthy diversions. You are constantly robbed often with no one to protect you; you are being discriminated against with no one to point out that your salvation lay in the retreat of your false conceptions. Who is there among you to realize it? How many remain to listen and understand the truth? For who permitted you to be downtrodden and Israel to be forsaken? Isn't it I, the very God to whom you have sinned, in whose ways you did not follow, and in whose precepts you did not care to abide? And wasn't it only then that I lost my restraint and let loose the rigors of war until you have been surrounded in the midst of towering flames with no avenue of escape in view and seared in its unbearable heat without realizing your shortcomings."

But so said God, the Almighty, who placed His confidence in Jacob and fate in Israel:

"Don't fear for I shall ultimately liberate you, just call to me and see how quickly I will respond, even if you will find yourself in deep waters I will be with you and stormy rivers shall not overwhelm you. In the midst of fire you shall not be burned and flames shall not penetrate you, for I, God, the preserver of Israel, am your protector. I personally will pay your ransom and prove to other nations your true worth.

"It doesn't matter how many dislike you, but in my eyes you prove worthy, and I love you, and I will convince people with your true intentions and the nations of the world with your spiritual mission. So don't fear, for even in the darkest times I am still with you, and the day will come when I will bring your children from the East and gather them from the West, those from the North I will reclaim and the underprivileged from the South I will console, from the end of the earth I will affect their spiritual reunion.

"And it will be then that it will be realized that every human being is the masterwork of my hand and the image of my design, and it will also be taken when my nation so blind will discover eyes that did not see and that they were deaf though they were capable of listening and intercepting my message.

"And it shall come to pass that all nations will follow your lead and all races will work in union, and people will wonder and say, 'Who could have foreseen such a change and forestalled such a turn of events?'

"But facts cannot lie, and they shall bear witness for themselves, and all will listen and say, 'Yes, it is the truth!' And you, Israel, will be forced to admit that I was right in entrusting my mission to you.

"And so, bear in mind, have faith and understand that I, God, am eternal, before me none was in existence, and after me nothing will remain."

IX

Cars in My Life

As I envision my bygone yesteryears, I so clearly see their outlined pattern entailing a most meaningful message. My phenomenal confrontation with car accidents added to so many mysteries that truly baffle my mind.

I bought my first car, a Dodge Sedan, in the fall of 1921 since I resided in Mount Carmel with my business being in Shamokin and could not depend adequately on public transportation.

I had only had a few days of driving experience when I left the store somewhat earlier so I could get to Mount Carmel before sunset in time for the Yom Kippur Eve services to begin.

On the busy corners of Shamokin and Independence Streets the Reading and Pennsylvania Railroad lines converge their tracks, making it a most hazardous point to cross. As I neared it the crossing watchman hastened from his sentry booth as he heard the distant sound of an oncoming train while people began rushing to cross the tracks before the gates were lowered.

I had just completed making the turn to Independence Street when someone darted in front of me. In order to prevent running over him, I drove the car on the sidewalk just as a mother wheeled her wide carriage with infant twins by. The car hit the carriage, overturning it on the street curb, then traveling on to smash the window of the Little Giant meat market, stopping right by the store's entrance.

A large crowd soon gathered with a hysterical mother exclaiming; "My babies, oh gracious Lord, please save my babies!"

The police shortly arrived and fortunately also two doctors who happened to pass there at that time. They tenderly carried the twins in a nearby ladies' hat store where they minutely checked on their condition.

Someone parked my car, which had sustained little damage, at the curb while I remained with the doctors to learn the results of their examination.

After about fifteen minutes' time the doctors assured the mother that there was not a scratch or sign of any mark on them, and barring unforseen developments they were as perfect as they could be.

"This is a miracle if I ever saw one," said Doctor Strickland. "It's if an angel were in waiting at the sidewalk curb to reach for them before they struck the ground," he emphasized.

As the crowd slowly dispersed I heard someone say, "this man surely is lucky, he must have done something good to deserve such a miracle."

In the traumatic moment of the shocking excitement I did not realize the full import of the Lord's gracious blessing to me, but as I devotedly prayed in the Yom Kippur Eve services, I inspiringly dedicated myself to the gracious universal creator.

I was not going to tell anyone of my tormenting experience, but someone who read the story in the Mount Carmel paper related it to the family. Thus we shared it together, the grief as well as the happy ending, on this momentous Yom Kippur day (atonement day).

The following morning I called the mother of the twins, asking her how everything was, and she joyfully exclaimed, "It's just glorious that everything turned out so well," while I promised her to remember them on their birthdays with appropriate gifts.

My second close call with a car was when I had it parked on Commerce Street, too close to the railroad tracks, and was preparing to drive away when a freight train caught the right side of the car, actually ripping it apart. Here again I did not get even a scratch, though the car proved to be a total loss.

The next terrifying experience I had with cars was on a snowy winter day in January. There was nearly a foot of snow on the ground and it was still falling when I turned from Independence Street into Water Street which parallels the Reading Railroad tracks.

Stuck in the groovy snow furrows I was following, I could not turn away when a thundering eighty-car freight train connected with the bumper of my Buick Sedan. It turned the car completely around and the car struck a cement wall, which was demolished, and then hit the rear of my shoestore damaging it extensively.

The ponderous train came to a grinding stop with the crew hastening over to check the results of that terrifying impact. They were astonished to see me getting out of the car without even a finger scratch, standing amid the demolition that surrounded us. Truly another serious accident with such a miraculous ending.

I did not keep a daily diary of my life, but this incident I am going to relate was indeed a most frightening experience.

One Sunday Fannie and I visited the graves of my parents at Mount Judah cemetary in Brooklyn. On our way home an old beat-up car crowded with nine colored people passed a stop sign and hit us squarely crushing one side including the door. The passengers in the other car piled out blaming us and threatened us with physical violence. There were eyewitnesses to the accident, but it seems no one dared to contradict their excited denunciations.

With the arrival of police, a semblance of order was restored and, as they left shouting derogatory remarks, I got busy finding out if we could make it back home in the condition our car was in.

The police directed us to a garage across the avenue and the men informed me that the car's body was bent, but the engine and tires were all right. They then wired the door that would not close and told us that, if we took our time, we might make it home with hopes and prayers.

It proved to be a more difficult task than I anticipated, for we had to stop several times to tighten the loosening wires and the rattling door became unbearable nervewracking. When we got home, three hours later than it usually takes, the garage mechanic where we kept our car offered me an unqualified medal for patience and perserverence and he designated the car without any wavering qualms for a regional junk yard.

Another incredible instance where destiny would for some mysterious reason test me with reverses but spare me physical harm happened as follows:

On a rainy day when Fannie and I returned home from a visit to Long Island our car stalled on one of New York's busiest crossroads, by the entrance to the Brooklyn Bridge. Trucks, trailers, buses, untold cars and vehicles tried to get around me, madly sounding their horns and giving me the good-for-nothing once-over look as they passed me by.

Traffic police tried to get the lines moving and also summoned a mechanic from a nearby gas station to see what was wrong.

After a brief checkup he said, "Buddy, I can start the ignition but once it stops again, you will be indeed in real trouble." "What are the prospects of covering one hundred and sixty miles to my home in Shamokin?" I inquired. "About the same chances as winning the Irish Sweepstakes," he readily replied.

Having nothing to lose but the present trying situation, he started it up and I ventured on the Irish Sweepstakes luck to try my chances.

Getting out of the street was a grinding test, then came passing tunnels, bridges, toll booths and numerous traffic lights. I kept on putting the car in and out of gear to prevent interfering with the ignition spark.

Getting about halfway home to Easton, I started to count the familiar names of the towns I was passing as if that would ease my problem.

All the while there was hardly a word exchanged between Fannie and me for fear it would divert my attention from nurturing the spark that kept the car alive.

Getting to Tamaqua, I considered it achieving a landmark accomplishment. Then came Mahanoy City, Shenandoah, Girardsville, Ashland, Mount Carmel, and we breathed a sign of relief.

"Zelikel (my nick-name), we made it," exclaimed Fannie as we reached the corner of Sunbury and Shamokin Streets, two blocks from where we lived, and it was right there that we found ourselves out of gas, but now it did not matter.

A gas station nearby took charge of the car while we walked the few blocks home with a joyful feeling as if we had just conquered the world.

"How does it feel winning the Irish Sweepstakes?" jested Fannie. "In a way it means more than that to me, for I have accepted a daring challenge and triumphed—this I consider priceless," I stated.

In recalling my many close calls with cars, this one I will now relate was one of the most frightening.

The mid July day rose hot and muggy as Fannie, my two sons and I left Shamokin on our way to Syosset, Long Island.

The air conditioner in the Hudson car was out of commission so we had the windows open but steamy humid air kept on blowing.

When we got to New York, the stench of gas exhaust and polluted carbon monoxide formed an opaque haze. The boys felt drowsy and drifted into a slumber with conditions becoming almost unbearable as we were entering the Holland Tunnel. Suddenly we all responded to the shrilling sounds of a policeman's whistle the reverberating echoes of which must have been heard on the other side of the tunnel.

The policeman lost no time stopping traffic as he excitedly exclaimed that we were suicidal entering the tunnel's exit.

He seemed as bewildered by the sight as we were. Cautiously he directed us to park at the emergency side platform where he checked our documents, made certain we had no drinking problem and stood near the car for a while, seemingly in deep meditation.

"I am not going to cite you for any violations," he calmly said, and before I even had an opportunity to thank him for such kind consideration he continued to say, "undoubtedly a gracious Lord watches over you and I don't feel as though it is for me to judge this terrifying action." We thanked him profusely for his kindness as he directed us to re-enter the Lincoln Tunnel.

Strangely everyone now became fully alert. There was not a trace of drowsiness in spite of the suffocating humidity, for it felt so good to be well and alive.

Gratefully I thought that my watchful heavenly angel had again not failed me, and for those Divine blessings I would be forever thankful to a gracious almighty.

Inadvertently I now remembered King David's sayings in Psalm 34: "There are some who may meet with many afflictions remaining yet without any serious complications, while others stricken but once result in fatal consequences to follow."

Though there may be some other incidents to relate, I will conclude the series of "cars in my life" with the following episode.

In the year 1968 Fannie entered a period when a terminal illness made everyday precious, so I decided to sell my Mount Carmel store, which would enable me to give her deserved attention.

It was also important for me to turn my stock into cash to clear outstanding bills and start liquid savings as a means of future financial security.

It was just about two weeks before the start of that sale when I was on my way from Shamokin to Mount Carmel and I decided to return and get something I forgot to take when I left.

On Maysville Hill I waited for a huge truck to pass and then made a U turn when a fast-moving car, hidden behind the truck, hit me squarely in my car's center. I felt blood streaming from my head and a traumatic shock in the realization of what a serious injury would mean to me economically.

I was rushed to Doctor Justine's office in Mount Carmel, where luckily he assured me that the wound was not deep and should heal within weeks.

At the Saturday morning synagogue services I said a special prayer for the miracle of being spared the terrifying consequences of this near fatal crash, and the ability to fulfill my sales plans.

CHESS IN MY LIFE

In my birthplace, the City of Grodno, one of our neighbors at Sakheim's Courtyard was the Chief Rabbi Zeev Margolith (who years later became Chief Rabbi of New York City).

There groups of young boys often played chess and in time I learned its rudiments and began to participate in playing with them.

One day a boy about twelve years of age (I was then seven) got a bit peeved when I beat him. He hastily set up the chess pieces and said, "let's try it again." Using the same strategy and combination, I soon mated him. Visibly angered he quickly set up the board for the third time and upon realizing that he was in a mating position he slambanged the chess pieces, scattering some all around the table.

Rabbi Margolith hastened from his study to learn what had taken place and, visibly upset when informed what occured, he sternly reprimanded him and then quoted the Talmud which states "those who indulge in anger are as if they worshipped idols."

I avoided visiting the Rabbi's house for quite a while at the thought that his tendency of getting easily provoked would again get the best of him.

It was several months later that I met with that violent wagon team accident and I did not play chess until I enrolled in the Talmudic seminaries at the towns of Stuchin and Meretz.

It wasn't until many decades later when I opened my Mount Carmel store that this fascinating game again captivated my attention. Of all the surrounding regional communities, Mount Carmel seemed to have been the most chess-minded. The one who was responsible for it was a person in his thirties who lived with a sister on the corner of Market and Seventh Street. His name was William Shindel (better known as Bill).

Lean but athletically minded, he broke his hip severely during an athletic contest at the Mount Carmel High School, which resulted in him being unable ever to walk without crutches.

In time he became an avid reader and admirer of classical literature and an addicted chess player. He taught many friends the rudiments and strategy of this game, and from morning until late at night his home became a mecca where any chess enthusiast who was in a mood to get in a chess combat was greeted with a cheerful welcome.

There were many teachers, other distinctive professionals, as well as laymen who took advantage of such a centralized setup, and during weekends and holidays, the Shindel home assumed the form of a regular club.

The sight was at times a vision to behold. Some would play just to pass the time interestingly with the enjoyment of an intellectual game. Winning or losing really didn't matter. In contrast there were some who would have every body muscle respond to the torment of the mind.

I remember one in particular. He was an expert bricklayer by occupation who when confronted with a crucial chess move would break out in a sweat, pining as if in childbirth pangs.

Those in between such extremes had of course their own modes of characteristics and actions.

A most frequent visitor at Shindel's was a successful Mount Carmel businessman who was a very poor chess player.

Mr. Shindel, being crippled, appreciated this person's kindness in taking him out at times, either shopping or on any other errands. In return Mr Shindel would, to a certain extent, repay him by giving him the pleasure of deliberately losing many games to him.

This sensible, intelligent businessman never stopped wondering how it was possible that he could win from the club's champion player and lose to many who were yet to win one single game from Mr. Shindel.

Almost everyone there knew the plausible reason but he himself. He was probably not truly eager to search for an answer that would rob him of the joy of winning games, which he really loved and which gave him so much satisfaction.

But mysterious, though, are the ways of God and two remarkable episodes occurred during the course of time to truly compensate him for the many good deeds he often rendered to Mr. Shindel and many others.

Once or twice a year the Mount Carmel and other regional chess clubs would combine to invite reknowned chess masters to play simultaneous chess with thirty or forty players, for which they were compensated so much for every player. Once the then state chess champion, Mr. Gutenkunst from Allentown, was the challenger and this Mount Carmel businessman was one of the opponents. At the conclusion of which Mr. Gutenkunst won thirty-three, drew two and, low and behold, had a shocking loss to this businessman.

Of course it was one of those unbelievable oversights by Mr. Gutenkunst that even a beginner would not make, truly a one in a million blunder, but it nevertheless resulted in added prestige for the businessman as being a worthy adversary.

But the most incredible episode was yet to come a few months later in the same Masonic hall where Mr. Gutenkunst had lost so astonishingly.

It was during a regional contest when about forty players of different towns were contesting for a regional championship. One board was played by Mr. Robbins, an attorney from Danville, versus a Mr. Fey from Hazleton. There was an urgent call for Mr. Robbins to return home so the businessman volunteered to finish the game for him.

Mr. Fey was rated a first-class player and, as Mr. Robbins position was largely inferior, the game was considered indeed lost, but to the amazement of the onlookers, Mr. Fey made one of those million-in-one blunders and the businessman exultantly proclaimed a mate.

These two miraculous repetitions of such monumental mistakes convinced me beyond a shadow of a doubt that it was a providential reward for one so truly deserving.

In the months to come nothing had changed at Shindel's. He kept on winning most of the games from Shindel and losing quite often to the others, but his two unexplainable, astonishing wins left their impressive, prestigious marks for many years to come.

One of the most remarkable events to leave its telling effects on me was when the chess master in blindfolded playing, Mr. Koltanowsky, played thirty-eight challengers in Mount Carmel.

It is a phenomenal wonder to stagger the imagination, for after the tenth move there are about four billion combinations and it doubles with every added move. The numbers then rise into the realm of timeless infinity.

For a blindfolded player to fathom such infinite combinations, his memory must keep pace with that boundlessness, and it was a wonder to behold.

Mr. Koltanowsky lost but two games and drew three, winning thirty-three, and it was that night when I saw the astounding glory of the universal creator in its majestic splendor in creating a human mind of two ounces of grey matter able to perform such magical wonders.

During the passing decades I attended quite a few state chess federation tournaments. Usually they were held in first-class hotels with all facilities for comfort and restfulness, but the one I remember best is the time when in 1941 it was held in a national guard armory at Gettysburg.

At the end of August there was a relentless heat wave, and with no air conditioning it was truly suffocating. The huge windows were opened for fresh air with flies and mosquitos having a field day. Yet this devoted group of fanatical chess devotees seemed to accept such an inconvenience with a sense of indifference as merely a part payment for a cherished game worthy of untold sacrifices.

For days the contest for the championship kept everyone's attention and suspense, reaching its climax on the final day when those remaining in the contest played for a decision.

Everyone seemed to soften his striding footsteps, speaking in a hush-hush and whispers. Often, after one of the finalists for the championship would make a move on the board, small groups would form to debate its merits, others would go to another room and set up the board's position to try to figure out if there was a better move to be made.

On the table where the championship was to be decided, Mr. DeCamilo, one of the finalists, was a sight of utter concentration.

Slim, round-shouldered with an olive-tinged profile, he was dressed conservatively so typically resembling an intellectual idealist. His autumn-brown eyes flickered with a sparkling gleam in tune with his engrossed thoughts.

Being diabetic he was plagued by thirst, and chess patrons kept on supplying him with glasses of water. Absentmindedly he kept up his chain smoking, and no sooner did he finish one cigarette when another was lit, the stubs constantly mounting on the ash tray, yet there was no unsteadiness as he reached with his pointed fingers to carefully make those important, decisive moves for the coveted honors of state championship.

I learned that he was employed in the garment industry and just about earned a livelihood. He probably could have improved his economic condition had he devoted more time to better himself, but such is the power of chess once one drifts into the cycle of its magical spell.

Mr. DeCamilo died at a comparatively young age but he probably lived in that short time an eternity measured by the devotion, idealism and utmost pleasure of that divinely designed game that has no equal in its magical, infinite scope.

This game of Oriental origin dates from about four thousand years ago. Its board has sixty-four squares, played with thirty-two pieces.

Since its invention, many have tried adding squares and pieces, others have tried to reduce them but all this upset its uncanny balance to make it useless.

The games played during these millenniums by billions of people number into countless trillions, yet no two games were ever played alike to a finish.

In my estimation, the inventor had to be divinely inspired. The game is a gift for mankind to enjoy with its mental innovations and demands for intellectual skill so endless in its infinite dimensions.

As in every field of accomplishment, chess has its outstanding masters who dominated its coveted domain but have many shortcomings in life's general activities.

Most notable are child geniuses in every field of science and human endeavor who are attributed often to the theory of reincarnation, their souls having formerly dwelt in other human beings in galaxies and worlds in millenniums past.

Truly it is one of life's eternal mysteries beyond the capacity of a mortal human to understand.

Similarly I often wondered why a person's stomach, whose acid can melt metal, does not destroy its own fibrous skin, and a human mind that has proven it could scale to divinely rising heights but could not lift itself at times from the very ground floor to grasp common sense and simple logic.

Dwelling on my chess life I learned in time that in sensible moderation it could provide a unique mode of pleasure and relaxation, as well as a tuneful exercise of mind, but if one does not have the courage to discipline himself, it may become an enslaving vice that could rob a person of the most valuable thing in life, priceless time.

X

Fannie's Serious Illness

As we celebrated our fortieth wedding anniversary in 1960 we could look back with a sense of pride and satisfaction on four decades of blissful accomplishments.

Despite so many years beset with seemingly insurmountable difficulties, our five children enriched themselves with a college and cultural education, a credit to themselves and mankind, and I now envisioned a well-earned vacation for Fannie and me to enjoy.

But there is an old Jewish proverb, "A mench tracht un got Lacht (a mortal human makes plans and destiny laughs)." It emphasizes the fact that fate is the one that makes the decisions and not humans. How truly literal it proves in life, I had occasion to best learn when in 1962 Fannie's legs began to swell.

Hastening to check this worrisome condition, the doctors at a regional hospital diagnosed it as phlebitis, but after months of precise medical treatment her condition nevertheless gradually worsened, and upon the advice of my son-in-law, Dr. Robert Karns of Manchester, Connecticut, an internal medicine specialist in Hartford Hospital examined her.

Shockingly we learned then that she was being treated for the wrong ailment. It wasn't phlebitis but the cancerous disease of lymphitis sacroma (or rather Hodgkins disease).

Being treated for the wrong ailment complicated this grievous situation so much more severely, which left our family so sadly frustrated.

In a get-together that very week we determined that Fannie must not learn it was a form of cancer and must be spared the vision of death constantly looming in her thoughts.

Clearly I recalled now the tormenting days of forty years before when, after a post-childbirth operation, Fannie remained for months in a dying condition, for many days not being permitted even a sip of water, and her feverish, seering lips were merely dabbed with moist cloths to alleviate the suffering. Then one such desolate morning, as I anxiously waited for the forthcoming report, Doctor Reese, his countenance beaming with a sunlit glow, greeted me heartily to say, "Ely, I am certain Fannie will live, for she smiled at me when I entered the room" Anyone experiencing such excruciating pain who can still smile must deserve the Creator's grace.

Now, forty years later, Fannie's life was again precariously perched on a dangerous precipice, yet no matter how I tried to encourage her, this time there was not a trace of a smile, merely a deepening shadow of contemplated forbodings.

In lonely evenings I depressingly meditated on what a drastic turn the wheels of fortune had so suddenly taken in such a short span of time.

The vacation we so dreamed of and planned for had so swiftly vanished in the realm of lost hopes and aspirations.

Taking its place was the start of making bi-weekly or monthly trips to the Hartford Hospital to benefit from advanced medical treatments.

Confidentially the doctors advised me that her life's prospects were but of two years' duration, but somehow I had intuitively felt much more optimistic.

That instinctive feeling brightened in the months to come when medical science made rapid strides in advanced treatment and a miraculous state of remission now set in.

Nearly always she went to Hartford by the Allegheny Air Line. I would take her to Hazleton or Wilkes-Barre where the flights originated.

While most of the year it provided no problem, it was so different in the late fall, winter and sometimes early spring.

On the rising foothills leading to the highest regional town of Hazleton, rain would more readily turn to sleet, freezing at times and making the winding roadways a virtual skating rink. Often when it only rained in Shamokin, it snowed in the higher elevation forming whirling drifts when reaching Shepton Mountain and beyond. More than once I had to return midway with my well-equipped car unable to make the treacherous grades. Frequently when I did succeed in outlasting the turbulent elements and arrive at the airport, it was announced that the plane's flight was cancelled because of inclement weather there or at the prospective landing fields, and the ordeal of returning home after trying so hard proved a most frustrating experience.

Such exasperating problems often repeated themselves when Fannie returned home and I went to Hazleton, Wilkes-Barre or at times to Williamsport to meet her there. The frequent announcements that the plane was late were indeed a distressing experience, for on quite few occasions the delay, due to fog or icy conditions, lasted nearly five hours and the torment of idly waiting became simply unbearable.

One blissful thing that lessened Fannie's depressing feeling and pain was her determination to continue helping in the store, usually by remaining all through the regular business hours.

It proved to be a most potent mode of therapy both mentally and physically, for being greeted by customers, "Hello, Fannie" and then heartily responding with a cheerful "How are you, Mary, Suzy, Ann, Lynda, John or Bill?" were treasured moments for her to behold.

While in the store she kept up her life's ambitious tradition, sending get-well cards to hospital patients, especially to those without many friends or relatives.

Such daily activities seemingly widened the distance between the virulent ailment and her urge to live a useful life, and undoubtedly they did much to prolong her life.

The most terrifying moments to experience were when suddenly a massive bloodburst or a convulsive spell would strike her and prompt hospitalization would be required. It proved to be an indescribable scene of agonizing horror and the twenty-mile ride between Shamokin and the Geisinger Medical Center seemed like a never-ending distance.

Such torment became ever more distressful if it happened in the depth of midnight hours. Being admitted in the emergency entrance amid the desolate silence of the winding corridors and examining rooms was truly weird.

Here the curse of entrenched bureaucracy emerged so vividly in the emergency room where every second counted and people's lives were at stake.

It was long past midnight when Fannie was once admitted, bleeding, vomiting and convulsing in chills while the doctor calmly questioned me about her age, family, her occupation and other similar technical matters.

Now Fannie's hospitalization at that hospital had spanned more than four decades. All he had to do was get her chart and all the information was there for the asking. I angrily reminded him that if the delay should prove harmful to Fannie I would not hesitate suing the hospital. His answer was that everything must have a system and, in general, they did not find it detrimental to the patients.

That night I paced the maze of shadowy rooms and deserted corridors, their forboding silence being only intruded on by the flitting steps of hurrying nurses or a forlorn moan of someone trying to draw attention to his plight.

It wasn't until the wee hours of the morning that we returned home and after proper medication the situation normalized itself.

CELEBRATING OUR WEDDING ANNIVERSARY

In 1963 the doctors gave Fannie a two-year grace on this earthly planet, so since 1965 every additional year was now sweet. And so, when I finally reached the momentous date of 1970, it was time to celebrate our fiftieth wedding anniversary and also the miracle of Fannie's life-saving remissions which I never thought would ever come to pass.

On Sunday, June the seventh, Fannie and I strode on the altar of the B'nai Israel Congregation where we so blissfully named our five children at their birth and solemnly renewed our wedding vows in the glory of Divine splendor and the Holy Scrolls.

In the congregation's social rooms nearly three hundred invited guests participated in a sumptuous banquet that followed the ceremony. Then came a glorious night of music, dancing, singing and wonder upon wonder. Fannie, whose life's termination was to have happened in 1965, was now gracefully dancing to the cheers and amazement of everyone around.

It wasn't until midnight when the assembled began to depart and Fannie, beaming with an enchanting smile on one of the most momentous days in her life, returned home with a prayer in her heart to a gracious Almighty who made such a miracle so splendidly possible.

OUR PILGRIMAGE TO ISRAEL

Right after we celebrated our fiftieth wedding anniversary it became evident that Fannie's remissions had become less frequent and the virulence of the disease more ominous, so I thought it was time to arrange the pilgrimage to Israel we had for so long cherished.

In mid July Fannie, I and two daughters, one a nurse and the other a pharmacist, left for the El Al terminal on our way to the Holy Land. About three o'clock we checked our baggage, certified our documents and made ourselves comfortable waiting for departing time, but Fannie got a violent bleeding attack, fearfully vomiting and drifting into semiconsciousness. Suddenly all our hopes, dreams and aspirations seemed to be shattered in a situation beyond our control.

The terminal officials placed a call for an ambulance, which swiftly arrived with orders to rush her to a Long Island hospital, but by the grace of God, Fannie's mind cleared somewhat, and when she was to be placed in the ambulance she protested that she was going nowhere but to Israel.

Our daughters also had the presence of mind to call the Hartford Hospital where she was being treated. They advised what medication was required in this momentous situation.

The official in charge of the El Al terminal operations, realizing our dilemma, gave orders to delay the plane's departure while he too consulted the Hartford doctors as to how to proceed in such perplexing circumstances.

Finally he was assured by the doctors that it was safe to let her continue the journey and with a sense of gratitude and utmost relief we boarded the plane with Fannie being carried up those high plane stairs with the departure now forty minutes late.

The churning of the plane's engines sounded now like the sweetest music this side of heaven, and rising in the grandeur of the stratosphere was truly a joy to behold.

When we blissfully arrived at the Tel Aviv airport, David Antibi, our prearranged guide, took charge and provided us with a most glorious two-week Israel pilgrimage to be remembered forever.

This most remarkable, agile and knowledgeable middle-aged guide made every minute count and no one absorbed their telling experiences more diligently than Fannie. In her own pragmatic way she was curious to learn all the historical details making this tour a period to enrich her life with untold splendor, but the most remarkable event that heightened its comparable magnificence was the fact that our youngest son, Roland, arranged to get married that week in Jerusalem to a girl from South Africa who was teaching in Israel.

Providentially the chief Rabbi from South Africa who named the girl at birth was then in Israel and was the one to marry them.

It is indeed so thrilling to envision that such a glorious and miraculous journey hinged solely on Fannie's momentous decision not to go with the ambulance to a Long Island hospital. Truly a Divine miracle to be cherished forever in its glory.

RETIRING FROM BUSINESS

As I previously mentioned, I decided to liquidate my Mount Carmel store in 1968, and like the usual trend in the cavalcade of my life the going-out-of-business sale was suddenly beset with unexpected problems.

It was ten days before the sale was to begin when my steady clerk with many years experience in my store fell and badly fractured her ankle.

A few days later two of my extras moved to other states where their husbands were employed, while one who helped me on special occasions got a full-time job in another shoestore.

I immediately advertised for help and to my dismay only inexperienced people responded. This unenviable situation proved most deplorable, for I still had a considerable number of outstanding bills to take care of and also the task of providing for financial security in my planned retirement.

Should this sale ever prove to be a failure it would indeed be a severe setback to my plans that I had for so long dreamed about.

Earnestly now I prayed that I be divinely granted the logical foresight to pick clerks most able to learn fast and get accustomed to the sale procedures in the short time that remained.

From the numerous applications I hired three girls in their early twenties. One was of Ukrainian descent, one Polish and one of Italian descent.

I then closed the store for two days to arrange the stock, mark prices and explain to the newly formed personnel how to go about their newly assigned duties.

Ann Kritzki, the Ukrainian girl, who was ordinarily employed as a part-time waitress, I gave the task of taking inventory as to how many pairs of shoes I had in the men's, ladies' and children's department. Also how many pairs of rubber footwear, mining boots, bedroom slippers and miscellaneous items.

I used to take such a general inventory once a year, which usually required my steady clerk about two days to complete it.

This time Ann Kritzki began counting ten o'clock in the morning and was done a little past four, so minus her lunch hour she actually completed it in the record time of five hours.

Gazing at her in sheer disbelief at the possibility of counting more than twelve thousand unit pairs in such an astonishing brief time, I asked her if it would be advisable recounting it.

"If there are any errors it will be insignificant," she assured me. "Barely more than several hundred," she added.

To satisfy my curiosity I got my Shamokin clerk to help me recounting and to my amazement it was less than two hundred pairs.

What really gave me now a sense of satisfaction was the realization that providence had provided me with clerks of proven efficiency, as the other two girls also had proven their proficient worth.

The sale proved to be an outstanding success, with the exception that I had in my inventory about three thousand pairs of rubber footwear and, at fall not having a trace of snow, none of it moved.

I called auctioneers for an offer and the maximum price was a quarter a pair, truly so shocking since some models had cost me wholesale over three dollars a pair.

That Thanksgiving Day the weatherman forecast cloudy skies

and some snow flurries which should not amount to much, but overnight an old-fashioned blizzard developed with an eighteen-inch snowfall drifting feet high.

Within a few weeks I sold my entire rubber footwear stock at almost regular prices and could have sold double that amount if I had it.

This unexpected snowstorm coming so early in the autumn broke a thirty-year record. Indeed a Divine blessing so miraculous and timely.

SELLING MY SHAMOKIN STORE

Upon my returning from Israel I fully realized that at best Fannie's condition was slowly but steadily deteriorating and that the time was nearing when I would have to devote myself to taking care of her. I then determined to liquidate my Shamokin store so I could devote my time as it would be duly required.

As with the Mount Carmel store sale, here too I met many stumbling blocks to impede my efforts.

My steady clerk of more than twenty years experience in my store had a breast operation, while another extra clerk who recently married moved out of town.

It was also at that time, seven days before the sale would start, that I met with a near-fatal accident on Maysville Hill.

But by the grace of a merciful creator I was spared serious injury, or possibly even my very life.

But it seems the greater the difficulties facing me, the more determined I was to make the sale a resounding success.

Contributing to such a determination were Fannie's plaintive contentions of recent years saying, "You know, Zelikel (my nickname), if God forbid should any misfortune strike you, the shoe stock would just about cover our outstanding debts.

"I shudder at the thought of having the children provide me with a supportive livelihood," she would emphasize.

And right she was, for it was only my well-prepared sales arrangements and divine help which helped to make this final liquidation a tremendous success.

When it was all over we felt now a sense of financial security, a cherished dream which evaded me and Fannie all of our monumental life.

MY RETIREMENT

A few days before New Year's I returned the store keys to the proprietor and for the first time in more than fifty years, I parted with a business address which was such an integral part of my active life.

Years of retirement should have really proved to be a cause of untold jubilation, especially after constant danger and perilous, manifold uncertainties. Yet the very thought of retiring left me with a nagging sense of disturbing emotions.

Somehow it seemed like a sidetracked pathway of wasteful idleness. It also in some way implied a dreary feeling that this was the last dividing line between precious life and the mystery of infinite eternity.

It was for that reason I referred now to my retirement years as trading a business career to that of a writer.

I now recalled the time when my grandmother on my mother's side, Merke, was stricken with blindness at an advanced age. She resided with a son on the other side of the town from where we lived. Almost daily I used to bring her dinner at noontime. She was frail, meticulously dressed in her cotton or woolen garments, and seemed the very personification of proverbial divine goodness.

In the summertime she usually sat longingly at the top of the second-story stairs. At my approach she heard the hurrying steps, turning her head in my direction, her face lit up with a crowning halo as I neared her.

Even before I ever handed her the dinner she kissed me tenderly and pliantly felt my face, moving her lean hands to touch my lips for me to adore them. A benign smile illuminated her graceful face as I affectionately touched it and kissed her lovingly, at times squashing a tear softly rolling down her face.

How could she be blind, I wondered, when her countenance was so aglow with such glorious brightness. She waited until I went down the stairs for the sound of my footsteps to cease before she started on her noon meal.

Returning home I evaded the busy city streets. Going down instead a secluded hill and crossing a wooden bridge over a swiftly onrushing crystal-clear creek, I would then reach the city outskirts in tracks of gardens and fields. There I would follow the musing sounds of the bubbling stream and dreamfully stroll to the tune of nature's magical whims.

It was on one of those whimsical strolls when I composed in my thoughts my first poem in Yiddish which I titled "Bynacht A Lain in feld (with night and nature by myself)." It was an incentive to continue such writing and at the age of sixteen when I left for the United States I had a considerable manuscript which I planned someday to publish. Unfortunately, when my meager belongings were stolen on the ship, this too was taken, undoubtedly useless to those who practiced thievery on the sturdy Batavia.

Arriving in the United States I was quickly drawn into the whirling cycles of life's unrelenting realities and my literary prospects became but an elusive vision.

Truly, though, it wasn't all a lost cause, for regardless of my untold trials and tribulations I succeeded in completing two novels now in manuscript form and hope to have them published when they are duly corrected.

I also feel a sense of accomplishment for having published in the course of many years over eight hundred letters in the metropolitan press and magazines, in which I reacted to the manifold timely topics and daily occurences of current events.

MY FATHER'S MOTHER

Previously I had an opportunity to relate my experience with my illustrious maternal grandmother while bringing dinners to her. I would find myself amiss if I do not mention how much my paternal grandmother, Freida, influenced the course of my life.

The family resided in a small town of Dubrovo and my grandmother's ambition was to educate her four sons as Rabbis. Her aspirations came to naught when her husband became terminally ill and she assumed the responsibility of providing a livelihood for her family. She was determined, though, that her youngest son, Joshua, should become a great Rabbi and leader.

At the age of seven Joshua was enrolled in a Talmudic school in Grodno, a distance of eight miles from Dubrovo. Having no transportation funds she started one day to walk with him that distance. It was right after the holiday of Succoth when a wet snow began to fall in this dismal late October day. Joshua kept on sliding and falling and grandmother Freida kept placing and replacing him continually on her shoulders, finally arriving at their destination as evening darkness set in.

In time this little Joshua more than lived up to her expectations to become one of the great Rabbis of our times.

This grandmother, Freida, was tall, walked proudly, shoulders upright, and was remarkably independent. When once asked if she resided with her daughter, her instant reply was that indeed her daughter lived with her (for the house belonged to Grandmother).

A short time before her death, at the ripe age of ninety-three, she asked for a glass of water so she could say one more Divine blessing that a drink of water required, and soon after turned on her side and placed her soul in the hands of her maker who had entrusted that spark of godliness to her for life's duration.

I often contemplated that possibly I inherited my sentimentality from my sensitive refined Bobe (grandmother) Merke and my perseverance and determination from Bobe Freida.

Unfortunately I was not privileged to know my grandfathers, who passed away while I was yet an infant.

CANDLE LIGHTING SABBATH EVE

I turned over the store keys to the owner on December twenty-first, the shortest day of the year when its end and beginning part and reunite in split seconds of providential timelessness, and the same week on the shortest Friday of the year I observed Fannie's Sabbath candle lighting that so magnificently sanctified the holy day.

On the wall by the candelabrum overlooked a painting of candle blessings drawn by a famous artist. Nearby on the dresser were saintly statues of a patriarch adding a glowing sacredness to this hallowed corner.

Fannie placed five candles in the holders in honor of our five children and devotedly cupped her outstretched palms by her forehead shading piously her partly closed eyes as she entreated the Almighty for her family's health, happiness and contentment.

As I sat on a sofa in the living room observing this inspiring scene it brought back thoughts and memories of times and decades which had long ago faded into the infinity of eternity.

One such episode I clearly recollected now as on an unusual, busy Good Friday with standing room only in our overcrowded store. Children were screaming, men and women pleading to be waited on with customers at the entrance trying to get in. The time for the prescribed candle lighting before sunset was fast approaching, so a perplexed Fannie disregarded the uproarious commotion and dashed away by the back door rushing hastily home to light the holy Sabbath candles.

Hurrying back to the store she joyfully thanked the gracious Almighty that she triumphantly defied business temptation and did gloriously honor the creator by sanctifying the Holy Sabbath day.

TIME TO REFLECT

Professor Burk is quoted as saying, "Give a good man ample idle time and he will go wrong."

It could be equally stated, "Give a busy man some spare time and he may learn what life is all about." This came to my thoughts that first Friday night with time for sober reflections. It was after the Sabbath evening meal. Fannie took her prescribed medicine, which usually made her drowsy, and drifted into slumber.

Overburdened, cloudy skies began to leisurely release snowflakes which descended listlessly and made the surrounding sight truly a fairy-tale scene.

Dreamfully my thoughts ventured now into the nostalgic realm of my childhood years and the world around us.

Mankind's means of energy consisted then wholly of animal power. Roads were largely unpaved and traveling any kind of a distance was a trying undertaking. Electricity as well as telephones was in its novel infancy, while such inventions as phonographs and gramophones were wonders to marvel about. Automobiles, then in their primitive stage, were questioned as to their practical usefulness, and airplanes as a means of mass transportation were generally viewed as mere wishful thinking. Radio and television, whose very names didn't even exist, were mere fantasy.

At the dawn of this century medical science had untold limitations. Operations and amputations as well as childbirth were plagued by fatalities, and crude anesthetics left much to be desired, especially with side-effects to contend with.

Stunning, of course, was the electronic and computerized age that followed. It came to the point where the scientists who knew how their inventions performed, had no conception at times of what made the elements execute their given missions.

On this hallowed Sabbath Eve I could not help but be thrilled by the Almighty's glorious wonders that came to pass in this miraculous century of astonishing accomplishments.

Most convincing to me of the creator's presence were the mysterious, unaccountable television and radio performances, truly fathomless beyond the capacity of a human mind ever to conceive.

Once when an agnostic neighbor of mine dismissed the Almighty as non-existing I related to him the miracle of television as ample proof of an everlasting creator.

If every inch of earthly space were taken up with television sets stacked miles high, and if each one were turned on with a different program, each one would yet perform accordingly.

The congested airways that are, besides those programs, filled with telephone conversations, telegrams and other communications would not interfere or disturb each other, I stated to him. And should those countless trillions of television sets be duplicated with radios, it would not matter. Did he ever even try to give a thought to such a phenomenom that overwhelms and staggers the human mind? The agnostics reply was, "Oh well!" actually abdicating a logical answer.

I now recalled a quotation by the famous German philosopher Immanuel Kant who stated, "How could a mortal human with about two ounces of brain matter analyze a creator who is wholly pure mind?" A human being would indeed have to be thoroughly gullible not to understand that the airwaves' miracle could only be engineered by a Creator of infinite mind.

Fannie asked me for a glass of water and upon my return stopped at the window, observing the scenic beauty. From our second floor I gazed at the slowly descending snowflakes which seemed to unite heaven and earth in a rare display of bewitching grandeur.

By the alluring glow of the street light I saw the colonial-style corner home across from us. For more than fifty years it had been almost always lighted, the ground floor being the office of a well-known doctor. He passed away about a month before at the ripe age of eighty-four and he had kept up his medical practice until nearly the end. His name was truly legend with countless tales being related as to his manifold humanitarian deeds. Even in his octogenarian age he continued the tiresome house calls and even responded to nighttime emergencies.

During periods of prolonged idleness in the mines or extended strikes, he reminded his patients that they could pay him at a later date. During mine disasters he would be usually the first to arrive at the stricken scene and often the last to leave the site of misfortune.

I now recalled a recent news item about a revised list of medical fees, the different arrangement for house calls and charges for the various daily hours. Its cut-and-dried technical terms somehow seemed to diminish its humanitarian intent.

What a story the house across the street was telling me now, actually millenniums apart from the ultra-modern economic aspects now prevailing.

With every passing decade it becomes increasingly more evident how neighbors get less neighborly and the term friend is so profusely abused. Untold families become deadly enemies over inheritance quarrels. News about children resorting to murder is truly so frightening. One begins to wonder what next.

It is a world, I now contemplated, where the treasured word of love is being ruefully desecrated, a sanctified word so often referred to and so seldom truly practiced. Terror is constantly on the rampage with greed and hatred motivating forces to whirl the murderous cycle with ever-greater speed.

The most terrifying fact is that people in general are accepting it now as a way of life, and the tendency of not getting involved has almost a dehumanizing effect.

Murderers are often freed for lack of witnesses who fear to testify and face possible retaliation. Lenient judges contribute greatly to the proliferation of crime, thus exposing the public to the hazards of ever-mounting violence.

That Friday morning I heard on the radio that there was untold jubilation on the nation's commodity exchanges at the news of severe crop damages in many regions. This would of course enable the speculators to make greater profits on the holdings they own. How demeaning, I thought, it was to make human disaster a base for monetary gains.

The Sabbath candles began to spasmodically flicker their convulsive flames seemingly sensing its approaching finality. I noted Fannie getting restless. It was really time for her night's retirement. I soon helped her get to bed and then returned to continue the trend of thought on this first Friday night with idle time on my hands.

THOUGHTS ABOUT CREATION

Friday was the day when God created mankind in his image, but evidently that mere spark of godliness was soon crushed by the inborn human traits of greed, jealousy and searing hatred. So the very second generation found Cain murdering his only brother, Abel, on the mere suspicion that Abel was a divine favorite.

Ever since then a divided mankind has made this earthly planet a bloody battleground where rivulets of cascading blood crisscrossed into countless streams. Endless wars, mass executions and practicing genocide turned its flowing streams into manifold rivers of blood.

Some scientists consider such human bloodletting as nature's way of preventing this earthly planet from getting overpopulated.

In the animal world the various breeds and species kill and eat each other, so in mankind it is performed by its different races and nationalities, but such a callous scientific way of thinking may soon come to an end in the nuclear age we have so monstrously created.

With the proliferation of atomic and hydrogen missiles and bombs, future wars will not mean reducing population, but rather total destruction. Furthermore in the future battles it will not be a matter of bloodletting, but merely thermal disintegration, many being charred into refined ashes.

On this hallowed Friday eve, I now wondered, how can humanity turn the tide that leads it since creation ever nearer the mighty floods and precipices of doom?

I instinctively felt and earnestly prayed that the spark of godliness divinely endowed in mortal human beings would now in the nuclear age be nourished and cultivated until its torrid flame shows mankind how cooperation and devotion could convert this earthly, bloody planet into the godly paradise the Almighty meant it to be.

Only such a rejuvenated spiritual brotherhood could in time lead a confused humanity to the splendor of ultimate salvation. It is indeed such a regeneration that may yet cause humanity to some day look back and wonder what a mental block it had so tragically tolerated in the millenniums past.

In this day and age of nuclear proliferation the miraculous wonder of mankind's ultimate salvation may yet come to pass by the grace of our merciful creator.

FANNIE'S DEATH

In July 1975 Fannie went to my daughter's in Syosset, Long Island so I could leave for a two-week pilgrimage to Israel.

Whenever I go to Jerusalem I usually check into the King David Hotel, but this time I went to the Central Hotel, strictly ultra-orthodox, where most of the eminent Rabbis and religious leaders make their headquarters when in Jerusalem.

The reason I made that change was because at that time I was writing a book about my experience on pilgrimages to Israel and I wanted to get impressions of the activities of that unique hotel.

During the following Saturday I checked out, leaving for Tel Aviv, and informed them of my forwarding address, but because the Holy Sabbath day was not yet duly over, they would not write or for that matter use the telephone. They thereby failed to record my new address and thus there was no way for my children in the States to know my whereabouts and contact me in case of an emergency.

Such a crucial crisis suddenly came with a ferocious swiftness when the next day, Sunday, Fannie was stricken with a massive hemorrhage. She was rushed to a hospital where her heart stopped, and after a five-minute duration she was about to be pronounced dead when a faint heartbeat resulted, finally reviving her. About an hour later her heart gave way again, but this time the doctors waited eighteen minutes before they finally pronounced her demise.

On the way to the hospital morgue a nurse felt a minute pulse beat and rushed her back for the doctors to check, which led to a miraculous revival of life.

Doctor Bekke shook his head in sheer disbelief and openly declared that such an unheard of miracle could only be made possible by Divine grace.

During all those agonizing hours, frantic efforts had been made by my children to learn my whereabouts, but to no avail, and the tormenting frustration became truly unbearable for them to endure.

My sons then hastened to call Israeli government officials, many of them their personal friends, and explained the trying situation.

Soon committees were formed to telephone hotels in various cities, and after many trying hours they finally contacted me at the Park Hotel, Tel Aviv.

Arrangements were promptly made for a flight to the States and I arrived there early Monday morning. The children who were waiting hastily rushed me to the hospital where Fannie lay in a deep coma.

I tenderly held her dainty hand and with my first uttered words she raised the eyelid of one eye and made an effort to lift the other. I distinctly sensed that she somehow felt my presence and almost imagined her saying, "Zelikel, I am glad you are here by my sickbed."

I am almost certain that she courageously fought back the angel of death in that miraculous revival so that I could come back from Israel while she was still alive.

For nearly three days Fannie lay unconscious while slowly drifting to the end of a lonely trail to meet her gracious maker.

A simple wedding ring loosely rested on her frail finger symbolizing so gloriously the splendor of an incomparable mother, while a faint, benign smile adorned her hallowed face in the last remaining moments of a phenomenal life.

I kissed her a tearful farewell as her soul was divinely departing into a blissful reunion with providential eternity.

THOUGHTS ABOUT RELIGION

After Fannie's death, I began contemplating the real meaning and purpose of religion. Actually delving into the boundless maze of religious doctrines and rationalization means treading on ground where angels fear to dwell. At best it is getting into a situation where one will be hopelessly devoid of an answer, but I aim to limit myself to some basics that seem to satisfy my beliefs and conscience.

Since time immemorial Orthodox Judaism has been the fundamental base of Jewish religion. Its tenets, codes and doctrines have been established in the Bible and implemented by the theological commentators whose biblical interpretations formed the colossal tracts of the Talmud. It became almost an impossibility for the average Jewish person to search in those voluminous publications for his various religious duties. The salvation came during the sixteenth century when the outstanding theological genius Rabbi Joseph Caro condensed all of the manifold doctrines and laws in brief and concise form, making it easy for even the most ordinary person to understand. It was titled the "Shulchan Aruch (a table prepared)" and it contains 613 tenets and codes which a religious person is obligated to fulfill whenever the opportunity presents itself to them.

In the seventeenth century there was initiated in Germany a new faction known as the "Reform Movement." To them the Shulchan Aruchs coded doctrines were to be totally disregarded. In their place the principles of ethics and morality were to become the basic foundation of Judaism with the traditional historical past as a mere decorative beautification.

But in the twentieth century it is the middle-of-the-road conservative denomination, that has captured the imagination of the majority of the Jewish people, which seems to be most compatible with the trend of modern living. Their fast-growing congregations are yet in the formative stage with the Shulchan Aruch tenets being decoded into what is considered most essential and those that can be dispensed with as being irrelevant.

I, as a descendant of a Rabbinical family, was raised strictly an an Orthodox Jew. From my early youth I was taught that one must follow the precepts of our faith without ever questioning their logic or reason why.

I followed diligently those straight and narrow pathways of Orthodox Judaism, but its roadway began to widen when I arrived in the United States. I then often questioned what were really the basic fundamentals in religious performance, and what are mere irrelevant summations that Talmudic scholars have added in the course of passing millenniums.

One of the episodes that greatly captured my attention was the following event.

Rabbi Shamai headed the theological academy known as "Beth Shamai." It was most conservative in strictly interpreting the Biblical laws. In contrast Rabbi Hillel headed the academy known as "Beth Hillel" and he was taking a most liberal view as to the Bible's intents and meanings.

Once a student inquired of Rabbi Shamai as to how long it

would take a person to learn the codes of the Jewish religion and the reply was that even to just understand them moderately one would have to study for many months. The student then went to Rabbi Hillel and asked him the same question and his answer was that it really would be a matter of minutes.

Astonished by such a possibility he asked for an explanation, to which Rabbi Hillel stated, "One can fulfill the spirit of the Jewish religion by practicing the virtue of loving your neighbor like yourself, for if a person will truly determine to follow such brotherhood and friendship, one would not kill, rob, bear false witness, spread harmful gossip, would not envy anyone who achieved success, and in time of trouble would gladly extend a helpful hand.

"Such virtuous performance is what truly pleases the universal creator and constitutes Jewish religion in its most Divine form," explained Rabbi Hillel.

Another event that deeply ingrained itself in my heart and soul was the following episode.

At the age of eighteen I attended Yom Kippur (day of atonement) services at a centralized Pittsburgh synagogue. Surprisingly I was honored with the distinguished privilege of being called to read the Haftoro (an epilogue to the Bible reading), which was the prophetic chapter of Isaiah 58.

It is a chapter where the Almighty tells the prophet Isaiah to confront his people; "Cry aloud, spare not the time, lift up your voice and point out to them their transgressions, and to the house of Jacob their sins. Daily they seek me in delight to know my ways as if they would really seek righteousness and did not forsake my ordinances. Why have we fasted and afflicted ourselves on the day of atonement without getting a favorable response, they complain. It is because on the very day of fasting, your thoughts are how to improve your economic standing. Your mind is occupied with seeking profit by adding burdens to those you employ as workers. Is such a fast to be chosen as acceptable? Surely not. Rather this is what the Lord prefers instead of such fasting. Loosen the chains of wickedness, undo the evil bonds of depression, let the subdued go free and break the yokes of tyranny. Share your food with the hungry and invite the poor to your home, provide clothes for the needy and never refuse to help your fellow men. It is then, when you will follow the providential virtues of compassion and justice, that the Lord will bestow on you his everlasting blessings, for this is the promise and the spoken word of the universal creator.''

Reciting that inspiring chapter of Isaiah before such an attentive multitude of worshippers on the Day of Atonement was a magnificent experience that left its lasting impression on me. Deeply ingrained in my heart and soul was the splendor of that immortal prophetic message that humanitarian responsibilities to mankind are more meaningful to the Almighty than paying homage and singing his praises.

UNBECOMING RELIGIOUS FRICTION

With the passing of years and decades I could not help but be aggravated and resent the fanatical intolerance which various religious factions have resorted to in order to justify each other's accepted contentions.

Time and again during bygone centuries they did not hesitate to use the awesome curse of charom (ostracize) to excommunicate the condemned from the very folds of the Jewish community.

Because of the enormity of its tragic consequences it is rarely practiced now, but the ingredients for such prevailing hostility still burn fiercely in the hearts and minds of such intolerant zealots, causing much grief and discredit to the Jewish people.

The arguments of those who indulge in such degrading tactics are that there is no benefit for them in practicing it. Rather they are proud to preserve the glory of the Almighty.

How ridiculous such contention sounds when the Bible constantly stresses the cherished importance of unity and understanding by means of persuasion and reasoning.

The fact is that tolerance, friendship and goodwill are the cornerstones of Jewish religion, and those who do not see that are left without a spiritual foundation.

THE TWO PARTS OF THE JEWISH RELIGION

The Jewish religion consists really of two parts. One is mankind's relationship to God, and the other is people's dealings with each other.

In regard to transgressions committed against God, there are several times for possible forgiveness. One such time is the Day of Atonement when a sinner who earnestly regrets his misdeeds will be pardoned if he devotedly implores God for exoneration.

This does not follow when one inflicts grievous wrongs against his fellow men, such as bearing false witness, spreading malicious gossip or other demonic acts that would result in grief, humiliation and at times ruination. Then even the Almighty God cannot forgive. The evil perpetrator must approach the unfortunate victim whom he so sadly wronged and ask his forgiveness. Yet the untold published commentations of how best to serve the Almighty and humanity dwell largely on mankind's conduct in the Almighty's adoration, giving very minimum attention to the humanitarian aspects of life which are so predominately important.

At the yearly Rabbinical assemblies and conventions, there too the themes of conversation and discussion are predominately providential as opposed to any fundamental stress on humanitarianism. Such trends equally hold true in prayer books which, in their zeal to glorify the Almighty, are often degrading to the Almighty's fathomless splendor.

Some of such unsuitable sentiments are: "The Almighty is a man of war," "He is mighty in battle," "He is powerful and strong," "He is a God of vengeance," "He is a destroyer of adversaries," "He binds Kings in chains and nobles in irons," and so on.

To me it sounds so demeaning to a Creator whose very image no human being has the vaguest conception of, or any inkling of the Creator's untold glory and splendor.

When I visit my children in other cities I try to worship in a smaller synagogue whenever possible. Somehow I find the extensive modern edifices devoid of a feeling of togetherness. Such a sense is especially notable when the services are poorly attended and the prayers re-echo in a glaring emptiness.

In the compactness of a smaller house of worship, group singing is so much more inspiring and the feeling of common fellowship so vivid and truly rewarding.

ULTIMATE FAITH

In the prescribed Jewish laws there are many instances when one must readily forfeit a life rather than commit a sinful deed. In the course of centuries, countless thousands stood the ultimate test, going to their death without a moment of hesitation.

I was reminded of it now as I recalled a year when at the age of twelve I spent my vacation with father in the resort of Lasosna.

On a sunny morning we took our usual stroll in the nearby Pine Forest. The blazing shafts of dazzling sun rays played hide and seek amidst the gently swaying tree branches while the multi-chorus of chirping and singing birds paid homage to the glories of a bewitching world surrounding us. Then, unexpectedly, my father stopped for a while and said: "My son, how I pray to God for an opportunity to give my life on the altar of his infinite glory." To this day it remains a perplexing enigma to me what made him think of it so suddenly. Truly it was a magnificent day when even the most unfortunate would feel like living.

Such readiness to make an ultimate sacrifice to the universal

Creator was largely induced by his youthful indoctrination from the very day a child's foot stepped over the Cheder (school) portals.

Such Cheder indoctrinations prompted me to recall the time when there was a change of Rebbes (teachers) and the first lesson was how to beware of women's enchantment.

The Rebbe was somewhat tall, lean, and had red hair with watery blue eyes. In contrast his wife was short, and had raven black eyes with a pronounced midsection as if in permanent pregnancy.

"You are now of age," he said, "when the wise words of King Solomon in the Book of Proverbs will prove a timely lesson.

"We will begin there in chapter five where it states as follows: 'Beware of a woman whose lips permeate sweetness and her mouth is smoother than oil. Yet her feet will gradually lead one into ruin with her delicate steps a proven pathway to hell.''

The pupils, sensing now invisible peril and the sight of hell, trained a hypnotic gaze at the Rebbe while I was wondering how a woman's lips could permeate sweetness while her feet were leading to the doorsteps of hell.

One student named Shmulke, years older than the others and physically even above that in development, kept on smiling all the while with the Rebbe scrutinizing him with his warning look.

Continuing, he recited, "Keep away from enticing women and the flattery of their tongue. Do not crave their beauty for their attractiveness ultimately spells ruination."

The Rebbe's wife moved a kitchen chair by the door to partake in that lesson with an overfed cat making itself comfortable by her side.

The Rebbe, ignoring the added pupil, continued: "Can a person play with fire and not get burned? Or walk on hot coals and not scorch the feet?

"Surely," he recited, "one will not despise a thief if he steals to satisfy his hunger, but one who commits adultery destroys his own soul."

The Rebbe's wife softly sighed at the very thought that one could possibly be losing his soul for such a provoking temptation, while the cat gazed at her for any sign of trouble.

Starting the next chapter the Rebbe recited how in an evening twilight a simple-minded man was enticed by a glamorous woman who after a brief conversation explained to him that her husband had left for a few days, which would give them an opportunity to make love safely until morning.

But the Rebbe sadly concluded that this was a blackmail setup that could have ruined the man's life.

One student asked Shmulke why, if she had a husband, she bothered strange men, but with the Rebbe gazing at him, Shmulke merely smiled understandingly.

In later years I recalled the time when Shifra Neiman first enthralled me at the age of thirteen with her passionate, torrid kiss and in the captivating embrace of her beguiling charm. At that time all of the cheder indoctrination seemed to have melted away in the magical spell of youthful infatuation.

I often wondered if King Solomon, the author of the Proverbs, ever expected others to follow the advice he himself had not followed.

A more impressive lesson in temptation came when I once visited my father and he lectured me about how indiscriminate women tantalized men and led them into total ruin. How careful one must be to avoid temptation which leads to dishonor, breaking up of families and all the tragedies that that implies.

My mother, who overheard the lecture, told me later that in the Marcy Avenue Synagogue where my father was Rabbi, two members divorced their wives and remarried others they claimed to love.

What hurt my father most was that it affected the lives of many children.

THE ESSENCE OF RELIGION

Now as to the question of what is the essence of religious conceptions, truly I envision it as a divine system where anyone who wants to take advantage of it could attach himself to a personalized god.

I have dedicated myself to that vision and my very presence on earth today is undoubtedly because of the Almighty's response to my trust in him and my pleadings.

For, looking back at my momentous life, I find it to be a continuous chain of miraculous events. Time and again I was confronted with imminent disaster when magically unseen bridges came my way enabling me to cross perilous streams and towering overpasses which appeared like fathomless chasms.

In that respect I was not only privileged to realize instinctively the Almighty's existence, but I actually saw and felt his marvelous splendor.

Being that God created mankind in his image and gave it freedom of choice, it is within humanity's power to utilize its god-given opportunities to make its earthly abode an indescribable, blissful haven.

In this respect every mortal human being can contribute his share by practicing brotherly love, kindness and friendship.

In my estimation this is the fundamental basis of religion, the spirit of joy, of fraternal humanitarianism. It is also my theory that every human being is endowed with a shadowy medium (call it a guiding angel if one prefers) that clings forever as a part of a person's soul from the very day of his birth.

Those who are conscious of such a divine medium can sense more readily a godly response to their supplications in time of dire need.

In my prayers to a gracious Almighty I feel a sense of reward in the privilege of being able to be grateful to him, for truly God has no need of any praise and adoration.

Summarizing my outlook on religion. I am not only privileged to sense God's glorious existence, but honored to actually see and feel his presence in a personal, communicative attachment. By creating this earthly planet as an experimental station to see if mankind can prove itself truly human, God made humanitarianism the fundamental basis of religion.

Realizing that there are untold mysteries in the Almighty, I reason within my mental ability as far as I am able and then abide with unreserved faith in the unabated truth and justice in the performance of a compassionate Creator. Such a religion has provided me with peace of mind and the thrilling joy of forever feeling God's presence wherever I am.

Index

Aaron (Nephew of Ely, son of Simke), 103
Abel, 201
Annie (aunt of Ely), 3-4, 11
Ashland State Hospital, 114
Atonement, Day of (see Yom Kippur)

Baird, Mr., (Ball Band Saleman), 85, 111
Ball Band (Boots), 84-85, 111
Baluta, Dr. Victor, 137, 142, 143
Bar Mitzvah, 5, 10, 11, 166-168
Bastress Lumber Company, 106
Batavia (ship), 18-19, 195
Bates, Erick, 31
Bekke, Dr., 203
Beth Hammedrerh Hagodel (Synagogue), 12
Beth Hillel, 206
Beth Shamai, 205
Bialik, Nachman, 21
Bible, 6, 166, 204, 208

Bolen's Auction House, 121
Boonshaft, Mr., 92
Bootery Shoe Store, 140
Buczko, Dr., 60, 142
Burk, Professor, 198
Burning Bush, the (Forward)

Cain, 201
Caro, Rabbi Joseph, 205
Central Hotel (Jerusalem), 202
Chapman, Mr., 92-93
Charom (ostracism), 207
Chekhov, Anton, 102
Chess, 178-184
Chachman, Mrs., 53
Chofetz Chaim, the, (See Hachoen, Israel Meyer)
Coal Township (poor board of), 138
Cohen, David (brother-in-law of Ely), 50, 52, 107
Cohen family (father-and mother-in-law of Ely), 27-32

Cohen, Louis (brother-in-law of Ely), 52
Cohen, Nahama (mother-in-law of Ely), 38, 48-49, 51
Cohen, Nathan (father-in-law of Ely), 35-36, 37, 45, 51
Cossack, 17
Crescent Shoe Company, 109

David (king of Israel), 23, 177
DeCamilo, Mr., 182-183
Deppen, Mr. (Millionaire), 150, 151
Dempshock, Victoria, 76, 106-108
Dickenson College Law School, 152
Dostoevsky, Fyodor, 102
Dubrovo (town in Russia), 196

Ecclesiastes, 124
Edelstein, Mr. (Auctioneer), 120
Ellis Island, 19
Ely's Sample Shoe Store, 139-140, 152
Endicott Johnson Co., 130

Farrow, Mr. (Funeral director), 121
Fendricks, Mr. (Constable), 119-20
Fey, Mr., 181
Firestone Company (boots, as compared to Ball Band and Goodrich), 112, 138
First National Bank of Mount Carmel, 151
Fleishman, Mr. (auctioneer), 119
Forman, Mr. (salesman for Firestone), 111
Fortney, Robert M., 151-152
Friedman, Mr., 110-111

Gabriel, the Angel, 57, 58
Galician immigrants, 125
Geisinger Medical Center, 188

Germany, 17
Gettysburg, PA., 182
Gettysburg Address, the, 29
Gladfelder, Mr. (Temple University Medical School Executive Vice President), 96
Goodrich, B.F. (Boots), 84-85, 111
Greaber, Mr., 47, 64, 67
Grodno (city of Russia), 1, (Governor of) 3, 11, 23, 24, 40, 100, 178, 196
Gutenkunst, Mr., 180-181

Hachoen, Israel Meyer (the Chofetz Chaim), 12, 13, 17, 25, 33
Haftoro, 166, 206
Hamburg, 18
Hancock, Squire, 147
Hartford Hospital, 185-186, 190
Harvest of Memories and Thoughts, (book by Ely), 151
Hector's Cafeteria (New York City), 83, 84
Hickory Swamp Mining Patch, 143
Hillel (nephew of Ely, son of Simke), 103
Hillel, Rabbi, 206
Hill Shoe Company, 91
Hirsch, David, 140
Hitler, Adolph, 73-74
Hoffman, Karl A., 151
Hummel, Minerva, (the Pow-Wow woman), 136-138
Hunn, David, (President, Hunn Shoe Co.), 110
Hunn Shoe Company, 110

Inzelbook, Rabbi, 38
Isaiah, 168-171, 206-207
Israel, 189-191, 193, 202-204

Janowsky, Reverend, 62-63
Jefferson Hospital (Philadelphia, Pa.), 95
Jerusalem, 191, 202
Johnson, Mr. (Temple University Medical School President), 96, 98
Justine, Dr., 178

Kallaway, Doctor, 137, 143
Kalmens, Malke, 11
Kant, Immanuel, 199
Karns, Dr. Robert (son-in-law of Ely), 185
Kashner, 149
Kelly's Inn, 136
King David Hotel (Jerusalem), 202
Kimmelman, Jerry, 74
King, Squire, 37
Klaus Synagogue, 23
Klein, Harry, 109
Koltanowsky, Mr., 181
Krehel, Peter, 152
Kritzki, Ann, 192
Kulpmont, PA, 157

La Cross Rubber Company, 111
Lasosna Resort, 7, 207
Latt, Oscar, 122
Latvian immigrants, 125
Lazarus, Emma, 19
Lermontov, Mikhail, 21, 102
Levy, B. & Sons (wholesale shoe company), 104, 167
Lewis, John L., 76-77
Liachowitz, Aaron, 134
Lighthouser, Mr. (Goodrich salesman), 85, 111
Lithuanian immigrants, 125

McGinley, Patt, 135-138
Mahanoy Mountain, 27

Marcy Avenue Synagogue, 25, 38, 211
Margolith, Rabbi Zeev, 178
Marion Heights, PA, 159
McKees Rocks, PA, 20
McKenzie, Dominick, 45
Meretz (city of Russia), 179
Merke (maternal grandmother of Ely), 194-195, 196
Military code, 13
Miller, Mr. (auctioneer), 121
Minsk, 12
Moonron, PA, 21
Moser, Fred B. (Northumberland County Judge), 147-148
Moses, foreword
Moskowitz, Rabbi Charles (father of Ely Moskowitz), 4-7, 10-12, 14-16, 23-26, 38, 83, 101, 174, 209, 211-212
Moskowitz, Cleo (daughter of Ely), 71, 94, 96, 115, 166
Moskowitz, Fannie (*nee* Cohen, wife of Ely), 27-32, 35-39, 43-44, 48-55, 57-62, 65-66, 71-73, 75-76, 79-80, 85-86, 94, 96, 99, 103-105, 111, 113-114, 152, 157, 160, 163, 175-177, 185-188, 189-190, 193, 197-199, 201, 202-204
Moskowitz, Frieda (First child of Ely), 52, 66
Moskowitz, Marquita (daughter of Ely), 71, 81, 94-95
Moskowitz, Meta (eldest daughter of Ely), 66, 71-72, 81, 86, 87-90
Moskowitz, Myron (eldest son of Ely), 66-71, 85, 93-95, 152, 157-159, 163
Moskowitz, Rachel (mother of Ely),

14, 24-25, 35, 83, 100-102, 174, 211
Moskowitz, Roland (son of Ely), 71, 83, 94, 96-99, 190-191
Mount Carmel, Pa., 27-28 (strike in), 32, 41, 45, 131 (shoeshiners in),
Mount Juda Cemetery (Brooklyn, N.Y.), 174
Moyer, Bob, 114
Muravyov (store), 1-2
Muskie, Edmund, 157
Myers, Senator Francis D., 95

Napoleon, 2
News-Item, 151
New York, 19, 41-45
Nieman River, 2
Nieman, Shifra, 9-10, 211
Nochum, Reb (called the Saint), 24-25
North Mountain, 54, 135

Ositko, Anna, 150

Park Hotel (Tel Aviv) 203
Pittsburgh, 20-21
Pivovar, Mr. (auctioneer), 119-120
Pollard, M.I., 33-36, 38-39
"Poor orders," 138
Proverbs of King Solomon, 6, 210
Pushkin, Aleksander, 21, 102

Rambam, the (Talmudic Scholar), 6
ration coupons, shoes, 91
Reese, Dr. George (Director of Shamokin Hospital), 54, 58, 59-61, 141-142
Ribner, Mr. (son-in-law of run-away shoemaker), 135
Robbins, Mr., 181

Roberts, Owen (Supreme Court Justice), 95
Ramney, George, 157
Roosevelt, Franklin D., 138
Rose, Dr., 186
Rosenberg, Mr., 33-34
Rosini, Mrs. James (wife of candidate for District Attorney), 158
Ryan and Ryan, Attorneys at law, 147

Salkov, Mr. (auctioneer), 118
Schwartz, Mr., 27, 69
Scott Colliery (the stike at), 160
Scranton, PA., 103
Shamai, Rabbi, 205-206
Shamokin, PA., 45-46, 61, 131 (shoeshiners in), 138 (poor board)
Shamokin State General Hospital, 53, 141
Shepton Mountain, 104
Shereshewsky industrial plants, 2
Shindel, William, 179-181
Shively, Sheriff, 69
Shmulke (classmate of Ely), 210-211
Shroyer Restaurant, 99
Shulchan Aruch ("A Table Prepared"), 205
Silver, Rabbi David, 79
Silverman, Abraham Isaac (uncle of Ely), 13, 20
Silverman, Meyer (uncle of Ely), 20
Simke (sister of Ely), 100, 102-103
Smigelsky, Dr., 53-54, 76
Smith, Mr. (ticket agent), 78
Smith, Lester (son-in-law of Ely-Meta's husband), 89-90
Solomon (king of Israel), 210-211
Spector, Sam, 119
Spencer, Dr., 144

Statue of Liberty, 19
Stern, Mr. (owner and publisher of the *Philadelphia Record*), 74
Strickland, Dr., 173
Stuchin (town in Russia), 11, 179
Syosset, Long Island, 202

Talmud, 178
Tel Aviv, 190, 203
Thomson and Crocker Shoe Company, 47
Tifereth Israel Cemetery (Mount Carmel, Pa.), 52
Torah, 3, 15
Touro Synagogue (Newport, R.I.), 129
Trachtenberg, Mr., 91
Tropp, Bernard, 40
Turner, Mr. (landlord), 61

Unger, Mr. (President of Market Street National Bank), 67, 70

United Mine Workers, 76-77

Vanity Shoe Company, 74
Vici Kid Shoes, 149-150
Victoria Diamond, the, 108

Washington Mills, 33, 36, 38, 64
Wardrope, Mrs., 53, 60
Wedding of Ely and Fannie Moskowitz, 37-38
Wedding anniversary of Ely and Fanny, 189
Wilkinson, Leonard, Jr., 106-108
Willoughby Avenue Synagogue, 38

Yom Kippur, 15, 48, 172-173, 206, 208

Zimmerman, Miss, 148
Zymbalist, Frieda (grandmother of Ely), 196
Zymbalist, Joshua (uncle of Ely), 12, 196